PREPARE
TO BE A
MILLIONAIRE

Kimberly Spinks Burleson and Robyn Collins

HCI
TEENS™

Health Communications, Inc.
Deerfield Beach, Florida

www.hcibooks.com

Library of Congress Cataloging-in-Publication Data

Spinks Burleson, Kimberly.
   Prepare to be a teen millionaire / Kimberly Spinks Burleson and Robyn Collins.
     p. cm.
   Includes bibliographical references.
   ISBN-13: 978-0-7573-0723-2 (trade paper)
   ISBN-10: 0-7573-0723-X (trade paper)
1. Teenagers—Finance, Personal—United States.   2. New business enterprises—
   United States—Management.   3. Entrepreneurship—United States—Biography.
   4. Success in business—United States—Biography.   5. Millionaires—United
   States—Biography.   I. Collins, Robyn.   II. Millionaire blueprints teen.
   III. Title.
   HG179.S55295 2007
   332.024'01—dc22

                                                                    2007052531

Publisher: Health Communications, Inc.
            3201 S.W. 15th Street
            Deerfield Beach, FL 33442-8190

R-03-08

Cover design by Sherry Leigh
Inside book formatting by Dawn Von Strolley Grove

To Tom Spinks . . .
a man who never stopped dreaming.

CONTENTS

A NOTE FROM THE AUTHORS

You are already there. You saw the title of this book. You raised your hand and said, "Yes, that's me." You opened your wallet. You really are prepared to be a millionaire. We are so honored to be the ones that get to help you make your first million.

The millionaires in this book have opened up their lives and their business plans to give you a look into their success. Follow their steps on a path of your own design.

We fully expect the readers of this book to be the subjects and case studies in our following books. We don't wish; we don't hope—we *expect* to write about you next time.

Until Next Time,
Kimberly Burleson and Robyn Collins

INTRODUCTION

As a revolutionary teen business magazine, our first priority is to provide relevant, cutting-edge information to equip teens for success in the business world. However, we recognize that to be successful, you must also have balance. This balance is what makes life rich and what makes wealth have meaning and purpose. It is crucial to incorporate compassion for others into your daily business plan. Awareness that with money comes power and that with power comes opportunity to effect change is what will set the truly successful *Millionaire Blueprints Teen* millionaire apart.

Be forward thinking, innovative, and diligent, and you will accomplish monetary success. Be brave, wise, and compassionate, and you will have acomplished true success. What goes around really does come around.

CHAPTER 1

Ephren
TAYLOR

From game developer to king of the world.

BUSINESS NAME(S):

Ephren Capital Corporation and City Capital Corporation

BUSINESS TYPE(S):

Private Asset and Equity Fund Management

LOCATION:

New York, NY

To sit down with Ephren Taylor is to enter the presence of drive, determination, and charisma. Taylor represents an unbelievably rich history of overwhelming success in mind-blowing rapidness. Getting into the game at the very "mature" age of twelve, Taylor was well on his way to the big bucks.

By age sixteen, he had acquired his first million. Within the next few years, he founded numerous companies. Today, he serves as the youngest black CEO of a publicly traded company and oversees millions in assets. He keeps his hand in many consulting groups and in various businesses—and he travels the country as a public speaker. He has a tremendous heart for raising people up and for building up broken-down communities, because Taylor puts his money where his mouth is.

A trailblazer from the beginning, Taylor is continuing to find innovative ways to increase community health and personal wealth. Millionaire Blueprints Teen sat down with Taylor recently to get the facts on how he has achieved phenomenal success as one of the premier financial experts of this generation.

GETTING INTO THE BUSINESS

So, you were making money when you were twelve years old?

It started when I asked my mom to buy a new video game for me. You see, we might have had the video-game system, but we would only have two games that came with it like Super Mario and some other Mario game. Anyway, I asked if we could get a new one, and she said, "Why don't you figure out how to make your own game?"

So, you just made a video game?

I was in the bookstore, and there was a book by André LaMothe about programming and developing video games called How to Make a Video Game in 21 Days. I got my parents to buy the book for thirty-nine dollars. I didn't realize you needed a computer, needed to know how to program a computer, and also needed an advanced understanding of math and physics to use the book.

How did your video game project start making money for you?

I stayed every day after school to work on the computers. I read that book over and over and over, until it finally began to make sense. I taught myself how to program computers. I made a game called "Clone of Pong," which was boring as all get-out, and an Asteroids knockoff. I decided to make a 3-D game; this was the last chapter in the book. Finally, I had created this video game that was as good as things out there at the time. Somebody saw it and offered me ten dollars for a copy of the game, so I started selling it. I wanted to be the next black Bill Gates. Michael Jordan was making ninety million; Bill Gates was making ninety billion—that's a big difference.

THE INTERNET

What happened next?

My work with computers alerted me to the miracle of the Internet. I knew there was money to be made, so I started a web development company, making $200 a pop for websites. My parents really thought I was selling drugs when I got paid $3,800 for two weeks of work. There was a company out of Florida that was contracting for a company in New York. They did health-care products for the World's Strongest Man Contest, and they needed a vehicle for selling their products. So, I built their website with e-commerce and everything. I applied for the gig with my alias, G-PROG. It just showed my skill sets (for example, C and C++ computer technician certifications, video game development, and more). They never wondered if that person might be only thirteen years old. I read so many programming books that my skills became expansive.

How did people find you to hire you?

They found me because I was on discussion boards and in chat rooms.

THE LEGAL

What about making it official?

I called my system Flame Software. I filed as a limited liability company (LLC). You can read books on how to raise capital, file taxes—anything. I was doing legal filings myself, because I didn't know any lawyers. I spent all of this time and effort to build this website for $3,800, but the people who used it got $800,000! I realized I was on the wrong side of the equation. I was just a techie, and I needed to be the owner of the company. I read more books. We couldn't afford Microsoft Office, so I programmed my own software. A company in Georgia started installing it on their computers.

So, that was in middle school. What happened in high school?

The coolest thing happened to me in high school. I had written this article asking, "Why should I work for minimum wage because I'm sixteen years old?" Every teenager thinks they need to get a job, but it's a rip-off for the teens. My buddy was running the school job fair and realized employers were paying a lot of money to market to high school kids. They knew that high shool kids were cheap labor, and that they were a good resource. We decided to create our own online job fair for teens. It would be a place for employers to reach their high school audience, and for high school kids to find out what employment opportunities were out there. We wrote our business plan on the back of our history assignment. Ironically, that history teacher was eventually an employee of ours. We started the 4Teens Network. We wanted to get employers to pay us to advertise their jobs online. At first, we had to give it away because we had no students and no businesses.

THE MARKETING

So, how did you turn it into a successful business?

Well, my partner was a white Jewish redhead, and I was a black Christian kid. We had started a business, even though we hadn't really done anything with it yet. We wrote a press release that told our story and e-mailed it to the media. That was before there were all these rules about spam. We spammed everyone who publicized their e-mail address. As a result, we got it in the newspaper every week for six weeks straight. We had nothing but an idea and a concept, but they thought it was a good story because of our presentation.

So, did this PR stunt pay off?

Public relations has helped me do so much stuff. Perception is reality. Because of the media blitz, we had 30,000 students slam into the website. It gave us credibility, and soon we were in business journals—like the *Wall Street Journal* and the *Boston Globe* where we got national exposure. Then we got our first check, and it was $35. I realized there was no way we were going to make a million dollars at $35 a pop, so I added two zeros to that for future sales.

What other marketing tactics have you used?

One time I called Pizza Hut. While I was on hold, I realized I had to listen to advertising. I talked to them and explained what we were trying to do. Because of that conversation, we were the first ones to ever put ads on the tops of pizza boxes. Also, we changed the name to GoFerretGo.com. We liked the play on words. Ferret means to hunt something out. We ended up making $3.5 million and having thirteen employees, including that history teacher.

THE MONEY

What happened next?

I was at an entrepreneurship conference and met John Vandewalle, a strategic planning business consultant to entrepreneurs. He asked me how much capital we needed to take 4Teens Network/GoFerretGo. com to the next level. My peer and cofounder, Michael Stahl, and I said $8 million. He tore my business plan apart, but I kept at it—making it better and better—until I ultimately became his protégé. I learned that the right introduction is worth so much more than money.

What happened to make you leave, and what did you do next?

I wanted to market to the urban core, and there was a difference of opinion. So, I left—and the 4Teens Network folded. After that business, I started doing information technology (IT) consulting. I was outsourcing before it was hot, because you could get people working 24/7 for much less. We built software applications for companies that didn't have an IT department. We would automate things and implement policies and procedures. Basically, we were the IT department for other companies. I retired at age nineteen.

You came out of retirement, obviously. Why?

In 2001, I started buying and selling houses. I would buy them for $10,000 and then sell them for $45,000. It would help the community. My wife's youth minister heard about the difference I was making and called me because he wanted to invest. He put in $100,000. I had developed an awkward style of investing, but my buddy retired on what his money made for him. I started the Christian Capital Group, LLC, which worked exclusively with churches and ministers. The average ROI for that company was 60 percent a year for some of my clients.

What is ROI?

It means return on investment, and, yes, it was 60 percent a year when I first started.

So, what are you doing now?

I am now doing private asset management, and we have a private equity fund.

Tell us about your proven investment system. Has it worked anywhere besides your hometown of Kansas City?

We tested it in Sacramento. We presented our plan to a group of investors, and we sold $2 million in houses in eleven hours.

When someone purchases a house from you for rental property, do you help maintain the property?

We have a credit investment program where the property management is outsourced in each city. With our insurance program, your mortgage is covered for two years if you lose your renters.

How did you expand into other cities?

In different ways, but recently we had a flyer at the Black Expo where an investor from Northwestern Mutual Financial Network wanted to set up an investment seminar in Los Angeles. Then, one time, a city council member in Cincinnati heard a testimony in church from a man who had been blessed by the program and got in touch with us about working in his city. It really boils down to people hearing about the success that other people are having.

THE SALES

We know that you launched a twenty-five-city Urban Wealth Tour promoting economic empowerment, affordable housing, and entrepreneurship in urban communities. Why did you do this?

The tour brings together private investors, educators, nonprofit organizations, religious institutes, and government forces to create positive change in urban communities. Also, I always wanted to get into public speaking.

How did you break into the public speaking realm?

I contacted Raoul Davis, an expert on individual and corporate branding. I told him my story, and he believed it was interesting enough. One of my first speeches was in front of the Congressional Black Caucus Foundation. I also interviewed with the International Speakers Bureau. They loved me. They broadcast to 600 members. I was booked for a Young Presidents' Organization (YPO) event. The YPO is an international peer network. At the YPO event, I was one of the highest rated speakers ever. We had no book, though, so there wasn't enough media attention. Raoul helped correct this.

How can someone attend an Urban Wealth Tour and get in touch with Raoul Davis?

For information about the Urban Wealth Tour, or about Raoul Davis of Ascendant Strategy Group, go to **www.ascendantstrategy.net**. To contact Raoul Davis, call 336-575-3594, or send an e-mail to raouldavis@ascendantstrategy.net.

What kind of money can you make with professional speaking?

Speaking engagements can be anywhere from $7,500 per performance to $12,000, if you hit *the New York Times'* bestseller list twice.

You are constantly looking ahead at new opportunities. What are some things on the horizon?

Historically, black schools have grant land that can be used to build facilities. We are working on getting biofuel plant construction on campuses approved. We are also working with Native Americans on biofuel plants. You know how old and beaten up lots of college dorms are. Well, we are in discussions to construct new student housing.

We know that you are focused on providing affordable homes for working-class families, thus allowing average families to afford the American dream. How do you do that?

I want to help communities so they don't have to lean on the government. I do a seminar on alternate revenue streams for ministers, in addition to my real estate project. But City Capital Corporation also manages assets and holdings ranging from large-scale real estate developments to bioenergy.

What companies are you currently involved in?

They are Ephren Taylor Consulting Group, Christian Capital Group (just for churches), Ephren Capital Corporation, City Capital Corporation, and STG Global Assets. I am part of Greenhouse Springs Water, Big Daddy's Fantasy Sports, and Extreme Energy Drinks. And, I just bought Investorsparadise.com.

Ephren Taylor's background in start-up firms—from tech to real estate and beyond—is nothing short of miraculous. He has helped start and fund seven companies, raising millions in investment capital. In 2002, his unique investment concepts earned him the distinguished Kansas Entrepreneur of the Year Award. His concepts on empowering local communities with both profitable and socially conscious investing and development, have made him a frequently requested speaker and panelist for events such as the Wall Street Economic Summit and the Congressional Black Caucus.

This "wealth engineer" is recognized as one of the premier financial experts of this generation. Some have said that his unique outside-the-box approaches squeeze every available dollar of profit out of each project for his investment partners and shareholders.

In his new book, Creating Success from the Inside Out: Develop the Focus and Strategy to Uncover the Life You Want, *Taylor actively seeks to educate others in entrepreneurship and finance and regularly donates time to speak for congregations and charities, sharing concepts such as "Vision Driven Wealth."*

THE PLAN TO FOLLOW

STEP 1

If you're interested in something, read about how others have achieved success in that field. Then, try it yourself!

NOTE: Taylor says, "You have to stay in your core competency."

STEP 2

Do your research. Read all the books you can on the subject. Teach yourself new skills. Be a trailblazer.

STEP 3

Go to industry seminars and events.

NOTE: Taylor advises you to find a mentor, and allow that person to help you forge your own path to success. He says, "Become their protégé. The right introduction is worth so much more than money."

STEP 4

Write press releases, and get your company's name in the media.

NOTE: Taylor says that getting your company profiled in business journals leads to profits by raising your credibility.

THE HIGHLIGHTS

- Don't let age be a factor in following your dreams of financial success.
- Utilize the Internet for research, for its discussion boards and chat rooms, too.
- Pool your resources (friends, teachers, online peers), and start your own company.
- Perception is reality; do not quit before you even try.
- Write press releases to bring attention to your company.
- Use creative marketing tactics to get profiles of your company in business journals.

THE RESOURCES

Ephren Taylor
www.ephren.com
Taylor's blog, where you can find out all you want to know about his speaking engagements and his numerous business activities.

Ephren Taylor Entrepreneur Camp/Academy
www.cheyney.edu/pages/news_article.asp?p=337&n=156
Specialized curriculum for high school and college students at Cheyney University. Studies include leadership skills, business plan writing, and entrepreneurship.

Urban Wealth Tour
www.urbanwealth.net
This is a multiple-city tour, with Ephren Taylor as keynote speaker.

Taylor, Ephren W. *Creating Success from the Inside Out: Develop the Focus and Strategy to Uncover the Life You Want.* Indianapolis, IN: Wiley Publishing, Inc., 2007.

City Capital Corporation
www.citycapitalcorp.net
Website states that they are dedicated to "socially conscious investing to empower communities." Ephren Taylor is chief executive officer.

Ephren Capital Corporation
www.ephrencapital.com
877-367-1463
Do you have financial dreams? Ephren Taylor's up-and-coming company can assist you.

Investor's Paradise Inc.
www.investorsparadise.com
Online stock market that offers investing advice.

Ascendant Strategy Group (ASG)
www.ascendantstrategy.net
ASG is a brand enhancement firm for individuals and corporations.
With highly specialized strategies, ASG creates, enhances, and promotes
innovative solutions to emphasize the unique values, images, and
messages of individuals and corporations. ASG produces profitable
brand portfolios. Raoul Davis (public speaking and branding expert)
may be contacted directly by calling ASG's headquarters at
336-575-3594.

Millionaire Blueprints Teen *neither endorses nor recommends any of the
companies listed as resources. Resources are intended as a starting point
for your research.*

SIGNING WITH BARNES & NOBLE

Landing a supplier contract with Barnes & Noble isn't easy. It takes persistence and patience.

Consider the case of College Prowler and its college guidebooks (**www.collegeprowler.com**). First, College Prowler became a vendor of record with Barnes & Noble (the publishing industry's term for a supplier), which allowed its guides to be sold through the Barnes & Noble website. (For details on how to do this online, go to **www.barnesandnoble.com/help/cds2.asp?PID=8149&z=y&cds2Pid=8383&linkid=472283**.)

Entrepreneur and chief executive officer of College Prowler, Luke Skurman, offers this advice: It's absolutely essential to follow all of Barnes & Noble's directions.

Here's the next step is getting books onto their store shelves. Barnes & Noble usually requires the use of a distributor or wholesaler; the company rarely buys books directly from publishers. Once College Prowler made a name for itself, it was able to set up an account with Ingram Book Group, the country's largest book wholesaler (**www.ingrambook.com**). Three months after being accepted into the Ingram system, Barnes & Noble decided to stock College Prowler's titles in its stores.

Skurman says the fastest and easiest way to get your title into retail stores is to hire a literary agent who will offer your book to prospective publishers. If you want to skip the agent route and sell directly to a distributor or wholesaler, as he did, be prepared for a longer road and more expenses. The College Prowler team chose to sell direct because it feels that being in charge of its own line could lead to more attention and greater sales numbers in the long run.

CERTIFICATION FOR MINORITY BUSINESSES

IS YOUR WOMAN- OR MINORITY-OWNED BUSINESS CERTIFIED? SHOULD IT BE?

Is your business at least 51 percent owned and operated by females or minorities? If so, you may be eligible for certification from third-party designators that will open doors to future profits.

Ownership matters in today's business environment, and women and minorities can, and should, obtain business certification, recognition, and approval when bidding for government or private sector business. What's certified today can pay off handsomely tomorrow.

Certification is granted by local and state governments and organizations. The general requirement is at least 51 percent ownership and operation by women or minorities. No figureheads are allowed. If this sounds like your business, you'll need to provide exact supporting documentation—a sworn affidavit is required, as well as a history of your business, including finances, management, personnel, legal structure, and more.

Certification can enhance your firm's ability to do business in public markets and with corporations that maintain diversity (for example, women or minority) purchasing programs. Although certification doesn't guarantee you'll get the business, it won't hurt. Think of it as one of your marketing tools that enables you to get your foot in the door. To accurately identify minority- and women-owned firms and operate with fairness in terms of their procurement practices, corporate buyers and government procurement managers often look for this official designation.

The certification process is not just "sign on the dotted line." Paperwork abounds—although it is made easier by the Internet—and you may feel somewhat overwhelmed. But the benefits can be well worth your time and money.

To get started, identify your customer base and then determine which certifications, if any, your customers require. Ask them, because there's no "one-certification-size-fits-all." Definitely certify if you're targeting large businesses (for example, corporations that subcontract or assign jobs to outside vendors) or the government. The federal government purchases more than $200 billion of goods and services from the private sector annually and is obliged to award contracts to small, disadvantaged, and woman-owned firms. State and local agencies have a quota to meet, too.

SHOULD YOU DO IT YOURSELF, OR HIRE SOMEONE ELSE TO DO IT FOR YOU?

Go online (use a search engine like Google), and you'll uncover a number of firms that will handle the certification process for you for a fee. Does it spare you from drowning in red tape? Possibly, but paying someone may not be in your best interest, according to Steven Sims, vice president for programs and field operations of the National Minority Supplier Development Council, Inc. (NMSDC). You are your best representative—the heart and soul of your business. "During our process, we want to really connect with owners. We want a real sense that someone is behind the business—that it's not a front company," Sims explains. "People can use lawyers, but when it's time to present yourself, we figure that if you have difficulty doing that, you may not really be the person managing, owning, or operating your business. In fact, you do have to be fairly aggressive when trying to obtain contracts.

"Of course, we know that some people are so busy trying to get their company together—they're not fronting for anyone—and they may require some help," he adds. "But when it's time for the 'rubber to hit the road,' we do expect to see appropriate individuals step forward and represent themselves."

CERTIFICATION FOR WOMEN

According to the Center for Women's Business Research (**www.womensbusinessresearch.org**), and based on data provided by the U.S. Bureau of the Census as of 2006, there are an estimated 10.4 million privately held firms in the United States that are at least 50 percent owned by a woman or by women. These firms employ more than 12.8 million people nationwide and generate $1.9 trillion in annual sales.

The Women's Business Enterprise National Council (WBENC) (**www.wbenc.org**) is generally recognized as the nation's leading third-party certifier, and is accepted by more than 700 major corporations nationally, as well as by federal and government agencies. WBENC certification can expand your company's visibility. Its special programs and initiatives provide certified woman business enterprises (WBEs) with information, training, and resources for growing their businesses. Members can access databases and participate in networking activities to learn from others what certification can mean for success.

WBENC's website is clear, concise, and guides you step-by-step through the initially daunting process of certification. WBENC has fourteen partner organizations nationally that handle WBE certification in all fifty states, allowing you to work with the nearest geographical office. Fees vary slightly among regional affiliates. There is a nonrefundable processing fee that ranges from $250 to $500 annually, so request cost information before you begin. Expect to wait two to three months for certification to be completed.

Along the way, you'll no doubt wonder why you're going to all this trouble. Because certification is worth a lot to its members, WBENC is careful to filter out businesses that are not woman-owned.

"I can fully understand what someone goes through as we're asking them to bare their business souls," says Blanca Robinson, WBENC's senior director of field operations. (Since this interview, Robinson has been promoted to executive director of the Women's Business Council, Gulf Coast.)

"Applicants are required to submit a lot of information that they hold dear and personal—and confidential. It's a stringent process, but we're very concerned with maintaining the integrity of certification. We can make no exceptions—everyone must provide certain documentation," she explains.

Robinson says that the WBENC will "look at the history of a business, how a woman came to own it, what her background is, and what she has brought to the business in terms of assets or financial contributions. Is she incorporated? What are her articles of incorporation and bylaws? Everything is used collectively, as a puzzle piece, to make sure the woman is not just the owner on paper, but that she is actually managing, controlling, and dictating the direction the company is headed," Robinson explains.

Sometimes, certification is denied. She cited a recent example. Two young women started a business and held 51 percent ownership, while a law firm held a 49 percent minority interest. But their agreement stipulated that, in order for the firm to provide funding and financial backing, everything had to be run through the corporation for approval.

"In this particular case, the women were very much in control, but they did not meet 'independent' criteria; they were too restricted. When they reapplied, they had bought out another company and were ultimately successful," Robinson says.

Help may also be available from the National Women Business Owners Corporation (NWBOC) (**www.nwboc.org**). Its certification is an alternative to the multiple state and local certifications required by many public and private sector agencies. Numerous private and public agencies accept NWBOC certification.

You can self-certify your woman-owned business at the U.S. Small Business Administration's (SBA) (**www.sba.gov**) Central Contractor Registration (CCR), the primary vendor database for the U.S. federal government (**www.ccr.gov**). Again, you'll follow the clearly delineated steps online. This is basically an honor system versus the more rigorous by-design programs noted above.

Many agencies or companies may require state or local certification, too. Again, ask the companies or agencies with which you want to do business, and they'll direct you to the source you need.

CERTIFICATION FOR MINORITIES

Start with the National Minority Supplier Development Council (NMSDC) (**www.nmsdc.org**), which was established to provide increased procurement and business opportunities for minority businesses of all sizes. Its structure is similar to both the main woman-owned business certifiers.

With a national office and thirty-nine regional councils, NMSDC has 3,500 corporate members, including most of

America's largest publicly owned, privately owned, and foreign-owned companies, as well as universities, hospitals, and other buying institutions. The regional councils certify and match more than 15,000 minority-owned businesses (Asian, black, Hispanic, and Native American) with member corporations seeking to purchase goods and services. As with woman-owned certification, ownership and operation by minority individuals must be at least 51 percent.

According to NMSDC, in 2005, member corporations' purchases from minority businesses exceeded $94.6 billion. Based on surveys compiled in 2002 by the SBA's Office of Advocacy, minorities owned approximately 18 percent of the 23 million U.S. firms.

A combination of screenings, interviews, and site visits establish eligibility—all under the supervision of a regional council. There is paperwork for this certification, but there is assistance along the way. Online certification is on tap for the near future. Joining puts you into the supplier database, encourages referrals to buyers, and offers access to ongoing education, networking, trade fair participation, and financing programs.

"The process can only be so simple," Sims says. "It must be rigorous to counteract the efforts of those who do not really own minority businesses but want contracts that reduce opportunities for real minority businesses. Unfortunately some have been very active in developing and promoting front companies and other entities that don't really serve minority business owners.

"Because we offer so many valuable services, the argument exists that, yes, owners should certify," he adds. "But some folks simply say, 'It's not going to help me.' Then some owners get certified and never participate. Remember: being certified doesn't mean that someone will walk up to you and offer two contracts that make you a multimillion-aire—it just doesn't happen that way." Sims is optimistic about the future, and adds, "There seems to be real willingness and renewed interest."

WOMEN'S BUSINESSES BY THE NUMBERS

According to the Center for Women's Business Research (based on data provided by the U.S. Department of Commerce, Census Bureau), the following reflects statistics as of 2006:

- There are an estimated 10.4 million privately held firms in the United States that are at least 50 percent owned by a woman or women.
- Women's businesses employ more than 12.8 million people nationwide and generate $1.9 trillion in annual sales.
- Fifty-one percent of all privately held firms are at least 50 percent owned by a woman or women and account for 29.7 percent of all businesses in the United States.
- Largest share of firms are in the service sector with 5.3 million in services, 1.1 million in retail trade, and less than 1 million in real estate, rental, and leasing.
- The greatest industry growth from 1997 to 2006 was in wholesale trade, followed by health care and social assistance services; arts, entertainment, and recreation services; and professional, scientific, and technical services.
- Three percent of all women-owned firms have revenues of $1 million or more compared with 6 percent of firms owned by men.

SPECIAL FUNDING OPPORTUNITIES FOR WOMEN AND MINORITY BUSINESS OWNERS

Did you know that if you are a woman, a minority, a veteran, a rural small business owner, or a small business owner of certain specialized industries, you can be prequalified for a loan of up to $2 million by the SBA? It's called a 7(a) Loan Guaranty, and the SBA even has people to assist you (ask about possible pilot programs for women and minority prequalification loan programs) in filling out your program application. These professionals can help you learn how to present your information in ways that make it much more likely that you will get the loan you need for your business.

Once your application package is complete, you can submit it to the SBA for consideration, and you will generally know within a few days if you're approved. Then, the SBA will issue a letter of prequalification that says the SBA will guarantee up to 75 percent of your loan. This means that if your business receives the maximum loan amount of $2 million under the 7(a) Loan Program, the maximum guaranty to the lender will be $1.5 million (or 75 percent). For more information about these special prequalification programs for women and minorities, go to the Small Business Center's website at **www.dsmallbusinessloans.com**, but keep in mind that this is information independent of the SBA. Use it as a research tool only.

A leading SBA lending source is the CIT Small Business Lending Corporation, which provides financing packages from $150,000 to $10 million to a variety of small businesses. To check out their resources for women seeking a business loan, go to **www.loanstowomen.com**.

There are also billions of dollars earmarked by the government each year for federal grants to minority-owned businesses that go unused because no one applies for them. All it takes, according to Government-Grants-Loans (**www.government-grants-loans.com**), is a willingness to apply for these funds at the national level—and keep applying. Multiple applications are encouraged. This web-site also suggests that oftentimes no one applies for them because they don't know how, or where, to find the information they need to apply. In addition to the site listed above, the SBA can help you gather your information for creating a winning grant application. An Internet search of "federal grants for minority-owned businesses" will turn up a long list of grants that may just be waiting for your application. In addition, most states and large cities have funding information centers that offer programs, workshops, and classes on applying for grants. There may be a nominal charge for these, but most programs affiliated with funding information centers are free. These funding information centers are great resources to find the money your business needs to grow. Many, if not most, of these funding information centers also offer access to the Foundation Center's (**http://foundationcenter.org**) national database of grants (called FC Search) through which you can search for grants that fit your business and mission. Funding information centers also usually offer many printed grant resources. To find a funding information center near you (many are located in libraries), search the Foundation Center's network of cooperating collections' (publications and supplementary materials) locations at **http://foundationcenter.org/collections**.

And for female entrepreneurs, there are reportedly even more sources for grants, loans, venture capital, and other kinds of financial help designed just for women-owned businesses (private foundations and federal, state, and local programs). According to Government-Grants-Loans' independent research, 500,000 women—this encompasses two out of every three new ventures—start their own businesses each year. They also state that women are reported to have a 75-percent greater chance of succeeding in business ownership than men.

Overall, the U.S. Department of Commerce, Census Bureau (**www.census.gov**), reported in a 2001 press release that the number of minority-owned businesses has grown more than four times as fast as other U.S. firms since 1992, increasing from 2.1 million to 2.8 million firms. Federal grant money for these groups can pay your expenses for start-up, expansion, and even legal advice or continuing education.

If you are a woman or a minority starting or running a small business, and you could use a little financial help to get your business to the next level, it may pay to check out the funding resources that may be available to you at federal, state, and even local levels. To get started, visit the SBA office in your area, or visit them online at **www.sba.gov**.

CERTIFICATION HELP IS HERE (AND OTHER RESOURCES)

Women's Business Enterprise National Council (WBENC)
www.wbenc.org
202-872-5515
Provides information on certification, events, regional affiliates, and more.

National Women Business Owners Corporation (NWBOC)
www.nwboc.org
800-675-5066
Certification applications, success stories, an e-procurement marketplace, and more.

Center for Women's Business Research
www.womensbusinessresearch.org
202-638-3060
Research on economic, social, and political impacts of women business owners worldwide.

National Association of Women Business Owners
www.nawbo.org
800-55-NAWBO
The mission is to strengthen, create, build, and transform women entrepreneurs.

WomenBiz
www.womenbiz.gov
Gateway for women-owned businesses selling to the federal government.

National Women's Business Council
www.nwbc.gov
202-205-3850
Advisers to the U.S. president, Congress, and the U.S. Small Business Administration.

U.S. Small Business Administration
www.sba.gov
Independent agency of the federal government.

Central Contractor Registration (CCR)
www.ccr.gov
The primary contractor registrant database for the U.S. federal government.

Business Matchmaking
www.businessmatchmaking.com
Matches small businesses with government agencies, contractors, and corporations.

National Minority Supplier Development Council, Inc. (NMSDC)
www.nmsdc.org
212-944-2430

Information center, statistics, regional councils, events, and more.

Foundation Center
http://foundationcenter.org
Search for grants through their database (FC Search), and find funding information centers.

Small Business Center
www.dsmallbusinessloans.com
Independent loan research tool.

CIT Small Business Lending Corporation
www.loanstowomen.com
800-713-4984
Resources for women seeking business loans.

Government-Grants-Loans
www.government-grants-loans.com
Independent research, statistical data, and links to grants and loans.

U.S. Department of Commerce
Census Bureau
www.census.gov
Provides statistical data and research based on national surveys.

Millionaire Blueprints Teen *neither endorses nor recommends any of the companies listed as resources. Resources are intended as a starting point for your research.*

Is Branding BS?

BY RAOUL DAVIS

It is one of corporate America's major clichés. Neal Lemlein, a premier entertainment executive and marketing consultant for the last twenty years, even asked the question as a professor at the University of Southern California. "Is branding BS?" he asked. Well, Mr. Lemlein, when it's a word symbolically thrown around as jargon and it doesn't come with a strategy, the answer is indeed, "Yes." However, it can be the cornerstone of a comprehensive strategy.

So, what is branding? Think of it through the lens of brand enhancement—identifying and analyzing brands for undiscovered or underdeveloped opportunities that will translate into consistent messaging, increased image, and profitability. Brand enhancement assumes all individuals have a personal brand and that corporations have a corporate brand, whether they have identified it or whether it is undiscovered. Another way to think about branding is to consider what you are best known for.

Speakers, for instance, need to spend serious time thinking about developing their brand before they begin marketing, developing their speaking topics, editing professional videos, and developing a personal style and their overall image in the industry. Too many speakers are motivated purely to make a profit. Or they are passionate about speaking but lack focus. Creating a brand strategy helps generate that focus—it allows others to see a consistent message and get a grasp on who speakers are and what they offer.

So, how does an individual come up with a personal

brand? How does a corporation come up with a corporate brand? It is done by creating a brand portfolio that identifies different areas for branding with corresponding imaging and marketing strategies, public relations implementation packaging, a product funnel, and a revenue portfolio.

For example, let's take Toyota. It has an overarching brand. Additionally, Toyota has Corolla, Camry, and RAV4, among others—all with separate brands and related strategies. Toyota is also the owner of Lexus, though you would almost never know. Toyota, wanting to reach into a higher-end clientele, must have realized that its brand was associated with affordable cars. Entering a vertical market where retail prices are $40,000 and up required the generation of a prestigious brand. Think about the market relevance here of what Toyota has done throughout the years. Whether you are a college student looking to purchase a cost-effective, high-gas-mileage first car, or you're a multimillionaire looking to purchase a third car that screams prestige, purchasing a member of the Toyota family is a practical option. Toyota utilizes very different strategies to brand its vehicles. Additionally, the cars often feature very different options and accessories. A Corolla purchaser may see cruise control as a nice option, while a Lexus purchaser would consider it mandatory.

Okay, that's cars. Now, let's talk about a striking example of a successful personal brand. One of the best brand builders throughout the 200-plus years of the speaker industry is that of the recently deceased Dottie Walters. Her "Speak and Grow Rich" brand is brilliant. The very name creates a crystal clear image. Walters's brand promises to teach you to speak and grow rich. Additionally, Walters had the seminar series of the same name while she traveled across the country, and she always carried herself with conviction and credibility. Walters' approach was to have a stand-alone name, "Speak and Grow Rich," which draws excitement by itself. Her branding has simultaneously been able to create an experience memorable enough to draw lifetime consumers who not only attend seminars and purchase books, but who also invest in her product funnel and become top targets for major symposiums and additional product offerings.

So, you have an approach and it's not working. Or you're attempting to create your initial brand. Think about some of the most powerful brands in the marketplace for the past twenty years. Consider Nike's "Just Do It" brand. When you hear this, it makes you just want to do it. This brand speaks especially well to the athletic demographic.

Snickers promises to "Satisfy Your Hunger," and when you're in the candy section after a workout, in between meals, or at the gas station on a long road trip, those words come to your mind consciously and subconsciously. You believe Snickers has an answer for your hunger.

So, is that what branding is about—simply coming up with a hot phrase? Absolutely not. Let's look at Starbucks. The coffee chain doesn't rely on a phrase, but rather on an experience. When you think about Starbucks, it is about more than the coffee. It is a place to meet friends, a place to study, or a place to just relax. Starbucks has been the sight for many meetings, dates, and breaks from the hectic pace of the day. This is what effective brands do: they create experiences.

I am chief executive officer (CEO) of Ascendant Strategy Group (ASG), Inc., and I want to help you get to the truth about branding. ASG is all about individual and corporate brand development. For one of our clients, Jeff

Johnson, a public speaker and social activist, we created two brands: "Social Architect" and "Bridge Builder." The "Social Architect" brand speaks to Johnson's ambition to create stable institutions that help people. Additionally, it captures the spirit of his keynote addresses. Johnson doesn't simply speak on issues. He provides tangible solutions. He creates an environment where creative energies flow, and one where the crowd is challenged to make its own solutions.

The "Bridge Builder" brand encompasses his ability to work with people of very different backgrounds. In his speeches, Johnson talks about the importance of people with different views working together. So, his brand speaks to his background and the experience that is created by his speeches. When you have this sort of synergy, it begins to make you a highly desirable and memorable speaker.

To create your brand, think about the things you are best at and what people compliment you on most. Create a simple message that will stick well. Then, think about the products that can be generated, including a website, books, CDs, and more. Make sure the phrasing generates an emotional image. Unless you are already an extremely successful speaker, the phrasing is critical. If you don't feel like walking through this process by yourself, consider hiring one of the many industry consultants.

Consider hiring ASG (**www.ascendantstrategy.net**). We are a brand enhancement firm for individuals and corporations. With highly specialized strategies, ASG creates, enhances, and promotes innovative solutions to emphasize the unique values, images, and messages of individuals and corporations. ASG produces profitable brand portfolios.

We place a full team around you; we are an ideas firm in the truest sense and specialize in personal branding. Our service has a strong track record for doubling, and tripling, performance within a twelve-month period. ASG has helped corporations improve their stock performance more than 700 percent and stands ready to help CEOs and public speakers ascend to greatness.

CHAPTER 2

Ryan
ALLIS

Took a company from zero to $1 million, and tells all.

BUSINESS NAME(S):
iContact and Virante, Inc.

BUSINESS TYPE(S):
Computer Software for E-Mail Marketing
and Online Communications

LOCATION:
Durham, NC

Ryan Allis took his first step on the path to millionaire status at age eleven, when he received a computer from his uncle. An entrepreneur before he even knew what the word meant, Allis immediately figured out how to use what he had learned to make some money. His early days of helping senior adults with the Internet for five dollars per hour were just the beginning.

After two summers of teaching basic computer skills to aging Americans, Allis's talents expanded, and so did his résumé. As a senior in high school, between cross-country practices and classes, he took a nutritional product company to more than a million dollars in sales with his genius Internet marketing tactics.

Allis left his profitable job with the company to attend the University of North Carolina (UNC) in 2002. Today, he is the chief executive officer (CEO) and cofounder of iContact, the leader in e-mail marketing and blogging software. Allis is also the chairman of Virante, a web marketing consulting firm that helps companies build sales online. He is also author of the book Zero to One Million: How to Build a Company to One Million Dollars in Sales. In November 2005, Allis was named by BusinessWeek magazine as one of its "Top Twenty-five Entrepreneurs Under Twenty-five."

Remembering where his company came from, he says, "We had a good product that there was a market for, but we couldn't raise money at the time. So, we bootstrapped. It took a long time to get to where we are now. It took thirty-five months to get to $1 million in sales, but, in the last twenty months, we've done about $9 million."

GETTING STARTED IN BUSINESS

So, you hired yourself out to seniors, and they paid you to teach them how to use the Internet. You also had a small business going that designed websites for companies. Now, tell us about the company that inspired your book, Zero to One Million: How to Build a Company to One Million Dollars in Sales.

I had written a press release on what I was doing and sent it to the local papers. On July 26, 2001, I was featured on the front page of the *Bradenton*

Herald. Five days later, I was in the business section of the *Sarasota Herald-Tribune.* Both articles featured Virante Design & Development prominently, printing the Virante logo and giving out the website address (**www.virante.com**). I had seventeen messages on my machine by noon that day. Every one of these individuals wanted me to develop their website.

A business owner saw an ad I had placed in a newspaper offering computer help, and he called me. I came to repair a disk drive, but it turned out he needed a new web designer, too. So, I ran to my car to get a copy of the article from a few days earlier, and he said, "So, when do you want to start?" He wanted me to set up a website and a system where customers could order his product online.

What kind of growth did you experience?

By April 2002, the company was doing over $85,000 in sales each month. In the fall of 2002, the company passed $1 million in total sales, with just one product and five employees.

So, since you were obviously making good money at seventeen years of age, did you go to college?

I made the decision to go to Chapel Hill, North Carolina, to begin my first year of college at UNC. Once there, I developed a network of contacts and built strong relationships that have been a great asset to me.

What networking opportunities did college afford you?

Right away, I discovered the Carolina Entrepreneurship Club. At the "Master Panel of Entrepreneurs" event hosted by UNC in mid-September, I met Jeff Reid, who was the executive director of the Center for Entrepreneurship at UNC. He suggested I talk to an undergraduate named Paul Vollman, who was starting an undergraduate entrepreneurship club. I e-mailed Paul. After we talked, he made me the tech chair for the club, so I was responsible for the website and listserv (electronic mailing list software application). About twenty-five students showed up at the first meeting. At that meeting, I was introduced to Aaron Houghton, a senior computer science major at UNC.

Tell us more about Aaron Houghton.

Aaron already knew who I was, as I had created a popular web discussion forum for the school that was featured in the school newspaper. He kept close tabs on the other web designers and developers at the school. We met, and he invited me up to his office the next weekend. His company, Preation, Inc., had been around since 1998. Aaron showed me a few of the software products he had developed for Preation clients. An e-mail list management software called the "Preation Email List Manager" caught my eye.

At that meeting, I agreed to work with Aaron to develop the software into a commercial version that would attract and handle thousands of customers. With software that met a need in the marketplace, my experience in web marketing and business development, along with Aaron's programming abilities, would enable us to build a profitable product line for Preation.

How else did you expand your network?

I started the Distinguished Entrepreneur Interview Series. To be interviewed, an entrepreneur had to be the CEO or the founder of a company that was doing more than $5 million in annual sales. There was no better way to build my own network, and increase my knowledge about what to do to get to the next level, than by talking with these entrepreneurs.

How did iContact get started?

I had been operating under the name Virante Design & Development for my sole proprietorship. But I was entering into a contract to market software that had a chance to bring in a significant amount of revenue—and I wanted to reduce my liability exposure, as well as lay the foundation for the company to grow. So, I incorporated Virante, Inc., using BizFilings (**www.incorporating.com**) as a North Carolina corporation. Then, I filled out Form 2553 from the Internal Revenue Service to elect to be an S-Corporation, which provides certain tax advantages to a small business.

Three weeks later, I received the Articles of Incorporation for Virante from the North Carolina Secretary of State. I was the CEO of an incorporated company, and my official company headquarters was located at 610 Ehringhaus Dormitory.

I formed Virante, Inc., to do web marketing consulting, search engine optimization, and to joint venture with Preation to sell the e-mail list management software. Virante would work to market the iContact software in exchange for a percentage of the sales.

We began building and improving the software. We came up with the name IntelliContact. The name was shortened to iContact (**www.icontact.com**) in June 2007.

THE INTERNET

What is most important for online sales?

If you sell your product online, sales copy is critical. If you will be writing your sales copy yourself, be sure that you emphasize the benefits of your product or service and not the features. Always address prospect concerns, tell why you are unique and better, and use things like case studies and testimonials. Always keep the acronym AIDA (attention, interest, desire, and action) in mind. Start by attracting attention. Then, develop interest, create desire, and spur action.

Do you have a certain process that makes Internet sales most effective?

There are five lead generation and conversion channels that the system is based upon. These channels are search engine optimization; affiliate programs; permission-based e-mail marketing; cost-per-click advertising (CPC) and cost-per-mille (CPM) advertising, and social media marketing.

What exactly does CPM mean?

It's a marketing model, referring to advertising bought on the basis of impression. This is in contrast to the various types of pay-for-performance advertising.

What is search engine optimization?

The most important factors in your search engine ranking are the number of times your target keyword appears on your homepage, whether the keyword is in the title, whether you have content on your site about this topic, and whether there are other related websites about the same topic linking to your website.

How can someone optimize the search engine experience?

By selecting keywords, ensuring that your site has those keywords on it, building good quality content on your site, and either writing articles for the site yourself, or going through the search engines to find related content. You can also outsource the creation of this content to copywriters using a service, such as Elance.com, for about thirty dollars per 400-word article. Then, build links to your site. I'd suggest creating a resources section on your site and placing your link partners in the appropriate category within.

How important is an affiliate program (where someone gets something for referring someone else)?

It seems that not a single successful online company is without one. The first step in launching your program is to obtain affiliate software. Most programs pay between 10 percent and 35 percent of each sale. Keep in mind that the higher you pay out, the more affiliates you will attract.

THE MARKETING

What was a crucial marketing move for iContact?

We created our first press kit and press release and mailed it to the editors of newspapers in our area. We were featured in an article in the *Chapel Hill News*, through which our vice president of business development, David Roth, found us.

In July 2006, when we reached a size that was large enough, we hired a full-time director of public relations. He has obtained countless podcast interviews and blogger reviews for us, the covers of *Fortune Small Business* magazine and *Success* magazine, a mention in the *Wall Street Journal*, in *Women's Edge* magazine, and in *CIO* magazine—and in all of the local newspapers and trade journals multiple times.

What marketing costs do you have?

At iContact, we have scaled our online CPC from $15,000 per month in June 2006, to more than $300,000 per month today. We scaled it in-house until we got to $150,000 in advertising spending, and now we have out-sourced our CPC management to ROI Revolution in Raleigh, North Carolina. It is important to be able to track your advertising back to the actual sale, so you can determine which campaigns are working and which are not. CPM advertising (based on cost-per-impression) allows you to purchase text and banner ad impressions at a cost per 1,000 impressions. Costs per 1,000 impressions generally range from one dollar to ten dollars, depending on how targeted your ads are.

What is social media marketing?

It involves creating interactive conversations with visitors, often through blogs, videos, podcasts, and social network communities. It is relationship building, not a promotional form of building your brand.

You can blog using tools like Blogger, WordPress, TypePad, or iContact. Some blogs utilize a tool like FeedBurner or iContact to track the number of their subscribers, as well as to distribute their blog posts automatically as e-mail.

Blogs can also utilize "widgets" that allow additional interactivity by showing information, such as the avatars (personas in the virtual world) of the community members (MyBlogLog), recent videos (YouTube), pho-tostreams (Flickr), slideshows (RockYou), bookmarks (del.icio.us), favorite blogs (called a blogroll), favorite music (Last.fm), social network updates (Facebook, LinkedIn, MySpace), what the blogger is currently reading (Goodreads), or what the blogger is currently doing (Twitter). (Other forms of social media marketing can be found in the resources section.)

Through all of these methods, you can go from being a company that communicates via a one-way broadcast tool to a company that builds authentic, open dialog in a democratic participatory manner.

THE SALES

What are some things that are crucial for sales?

Personalize the relationship, and build rapport. Once your customer develops trust in you, or in one of your company's employees, you are on your way to turning that person into a lifetime client.

Make yourself available, and answer questions. Although a phone call will always be more personal, e-mail can be a very effective tool for building relationships with your customers. If you can, be sure to answer your incoming e-mails with a quality reply and with quality advice.

Follow up with your customers, and send e-mails to recent customers. It's always good to give clients a month or so to evaluate your products. I've seen an e-mail double sales totals for the day it was sent out. It also enables you to continue the process of turning them into clients. The response from the e-mail will tell you how your product is performing, how it can be improved, and what else your customers want. It's also a great way to get wonderful testimonials.

What part of that is your job?

We all have to know how to sell via e-mail and via phone. We have to know our product inside and out, be able to answer any questions, talk on the phone with confidence, be enthusiastic, listen to the customer's needs, and emphasize our competitive advantages. If you can determine—and overcome—the major buying obligations of your prospects, you'll greatly increase your sales.

THE MONEY

How do you keep track of your finances?

You can use software such as QuickBooks, Quicken, or Microsoft Money to make managing your financials on your own much easier. But, as soon as you can afford it, hire a good bookkeeper. Later on, hire a chief financial officer. You may also want to hire an accountant to help you set up your payroll system and file your tax return each year. This will allow you to focus on building your business, instead of making journal entries.

iContact is a five-year-old, venture-backed, seventy-person company based in Durham, North Carolina. It provides on-demand software, making online communication easy. The iContact product is the leading e-mail marketing and online communications platform used by over 14,000 companies worldwide, ranging from small businesses to blue chip clients. Examples are International Paper, Ford, Bank of America, Super 8 Motels, Symantec, RE/MAX, United Colors of Benetton, Nissan, and LG Electronics.

iContact began in 2003 as a permission-based e-mail marketing application. At the application's core, it allowed you to upload a list of contacts that had requested e-mails from your organization, add a sign-up form to your website, select a template, paste in your content, distribute your newsletter, then view the opens and clicks, and manage the bounces and unsubscribes.

Today, iContact has evolved into an online communications platform that makes it easy to create, publish, and track e-mail newsletters, surveys, autoresponders, blogs, and really simple syndication (RSS) feeds. While RSS, blogs, and social media are becoming increasingly important methods of online communication, e-mail remains the top method of communication with your customers and prospects.

THE PLAN TO FOLLOW

STEP 1

Write a press release about your company. Distribute it to local media to gain credibility and new customers.

STEP 2

Develop a network of contacts, and build strong relationships that will become assets over time.

STEP 3

Elect to be an S-Corporation with the IRS. Earn tax advantages as a small business.

NOTE: You'll need to fill out IRS Form 2553.

STEP 4

Reduce your liability exposure, and stabilize your company's foundation for growth through incorporation.

NOTE: Expect to receive your Articles of Incorporation from your state within a few weeks.

STEP 5

Have interactive conversations with visitors to your website through blogs, videos, podcasts, and social networking communities.

NOTE: Don't underestimate the power of a personal phone call or an e-mail to develop bonds and trust with customers. Allis reminds you to be confident and enthusiastic, listen to your customers' needs, and emphasize your competitive advantage.

STEP 6

If you sell your product online, sales copy is critical. Be sure to emphasize the benefits of your product—not the features. Address prospect concerns, tell why you are unique and better, and use case studies and testimonials.

NOTE: When creating sales copy, Allis uses the acronym AIDA, which stands for attention, interest, desire, and action. He says, "Start by attracting attention. Then, develop interest, create desire, and spur action."

STEP 7

Make your Internet sales effective.

NOTE: The five lead generation and conversion channels that the system is based upon are: (1) search engine optimization, (2) affiliate programs, (3) permission-based e-mail marketing, (4) CPC and CPM advertising, and (5) social media marketing.

STEP 8

Optimize your search engine experience. Launch an affiliate program.

NOTE: Allis says you must select keywords and ensure that your website has those keywords in order to generate traffic.

THE HIGHLIGHTS

- Dedicate your time, and remain focused on building your business.
- Create a press kit and press releases for your company. Mail them to local newspaper editors.
- Maximize your social network by participating in entrepreneurship clubs, either in your community or at your college.
- Personalize interactive relationships with visitors to your website. It is crucial to sales.
- Determine—and overcome—major buying obligations of your prospects to increase sales.
- Track your advertising back to the actual sales to determine which campaigns are working.
- Keep track of your finances. Hire an expert as soon as you can afford to.

THE RESOURCES

iContact
www.icontact.com
Ryan Allis's on-demand e-mail marketing service. Build relationships with your customers by using iContact to create, send, and track e-mail newsletters, RSS feeds, surveys, and autoresponders.

Virante, Inc.
www.virante.com
Allis's other company, Virante, Inc., is an interactive marketing agency that assists high-potential start-ups and established organizations in launching brands and building sales online. Focuses on designing and launching integrated search marketing, CPC, e-mail, blogging, and online advertising campaigns to maximize web positioning.

Allis, Ryan P. *Zero to One Million: How to Build a Company to One Million Dollars in Sales.* Durham, NC: Virante, Inc., 2003.

Preation, Inc.
www.preation.com
Aaron Houghton's company that provides website design, branding, software development, and online promotion and tracking services for small- and medium-sized businesses.

Center for Entrepreneurship
University of North Carolina at Chapel Hill
www.ncruralcenter.org/guidebook/ViewResource.asp?ID=270
Direct link to the program at UNC that supports research for the North Carolina Rural Economic Development Center. Curriculum is taught by practicing entrepreneurs, venture capitalists, venture lawyers, and others.

MARKET INFORMATION

Hoover's, Inc.
www.hoovers.com
Want to research a company or an industry? Hoover's has this and more for free online. This website offers a profile database on companies, industries, and executives.

LexisNexis
http://global.lexisnexis.com/us
Provides comprehensive information and business solutions in a variety of areas including legal, risk management, corporate, accounting, academic, government, and law enforcement.

Factiva, Inc.
http://factiva.com
Provides essential business news and information with content delivery tools and services. Factiva's "collection of authoritative sources includes the *Wall Street Journal,* the *Financial Times*, Dow Jones and Reuters newswires, The Associated Press, Reuters Fundamentals, and D&B company profiles."

Zoom Information, Inc.
www.zoominfo.com
Search for companies, people, and jobs on this website, which states that it is the "premier business information search engine, with profiles on more than 37 million people and 3.5 million companies."

Dialog
www.dialog.com
This online-based information service helps organizations worldwide seek competitive advantages in business, science, engineering, finance, and law.

MEDIA CONTACTS
AND PRESS RELEASE DISTRIBUTION SERVICES

BUILD A LIST IN YOUR AREA. START BY USING THE FOLLOWING:

Vocus
www.vocus.com
Need public relations management help? Try this company's on-demand software. Also provides an extensive database of journalists, media outlets, publicity opportunities, analysts, and public officials.

Cision US, Inc.
MediaSource
www.mediamaponline.com
Known as the "leading global provider" of media research, distribution, monitoring, and evaluation services, this is your one-stop place for a media directory. The famous Bacon's Information is now Cision US, Inc.

Press Release Newswire
PR Web
www.prweb.com
Known as "a leader in online news and press release distribution," PR Web is used by countless organizations to increase visibility and user traffic and to improve search engine rankings.

Business Wire
www.businesswire.com
As the "global market leader in commercial news distribution," Business Wire transmits full-text press releases, regulatory filings, photos, and other multimedia content to journalists—as well as to the general public, financial professionals, investor services, and regulatory authorities. Also provides trade show and conference partnerships, and monitoring services. Has a reputation for being "the most comprehensive news and disclosure network in the world."

United Business Media
PR Newswire Association, LLC
www.prnewswire.com
PR Newswire provides "electronic distribution, targeting, measurement, translation, and broadcast services on behalf of tens of thousands of corporate, government, association, labor, nonprofit, and other customers worldwide." Use it to reach your audience, whether it's the news media, the investment community, government decision makers, or the general public.

OPTIMIZE YOUR WEBSITE

LinkExperts, Inc.
www.linkexperts.com
Purchase relevant links and ad networks. Advertising solutions are designed to focus link authority for industry-leading organizations with "unexpectedly poor visibility in organic search rankings."

ROI Revolution
www.roirevolution.com
CPC management company that offers Google analytics training, interface software, and Google website optimizer tools.

PURCHASE REVIEWS WITH LINKS

PayPerPost
http://payperpost.com
Consumer-generated advertising community. Offers online marketing, brand building, and traffic generation.

ReviewMe
www.reviewme.com
Advertisers can direct traffic, gain feedback in the form of reviews from bloggers, control messages, and track traffic and clicks.

Blogvertise
www.blogsvertise.com
Promote website traffic, and build links with this pay-as-you-go blog advertising platform.

TOOLS FOR KEYWORDS AND KEY PHRASES

Yahoo!, Inc.
Search Term Suggestion Tools
http://sem.smallbusiness.yahoo.com/searchenginemarketing
Customers search on Yahoo!, and other popular sites, and then your company's ad appears in the results. (**NOTE**: The Overture search term suggestion tool is now part of the Yahoo!®, line of search engine marketing.)

Google
AdWords
https://adwords.google.com/select/KeywordToolExternal
Use Google's AdWords (search term suggestion tool) to get new keyword ideas for your business.

Rivergold Associates Ltd.
Wordtracker
www.wordtracker.com
Want to raise your search engine ranking? Subscribe to Wordtracker, and learn the words people use when they search the Internet—and how popular each word is. This information allows you to optimize your website content with the most popular keywords for your product and services. Subscription also allows you to generate countless relevant keywords to improve your search campaigns, and research online markets ahead of your competition.

AFFILIATE SOFTWARE AND
OPEN SOURCE PLATFORMS

Website Pros, Inc.
1ShoppingCart
www.1shoppingcart.com
Offers shopping cart software, plus Internet marketing tools, merchant accounts, autoresponders, and an affiliate program.

Internet Marketing Center
AssocTRAC
www.marketingtips.com/assoctrac
AssocTRAC promises to make setting up and managing your affiliate program easy. Use this software to recruit affiliates, boost your sales, and be seen across the web.

KowaBunga! Technologies
{myap}
www.myaffiliateprogram.com
Winner of an award of merit for excellence in affiliate software. Offers tracking and management software, complete affiliate ownership, network exposure, hands-free integration, experienced support and service, and outsourced management services.

osCommerce
www.oscommerce.com
Offers open source e-commerce solutions available for free. Features an online shopping cart functionality that allows store owners to set up, run, and maintain their online stores with ease and with "no limitations involved."

HAVE CUSTOM SOFTWARE DEVELOPED, OR JOIN AN AFFILIATE NETWORK THAT PROVIDES BOTH THE SOFTWARE AND THE CONNECTION TO ADVERTISERS WHO CAN PROMOTE YOUR PRODUCT.

Commission Junction, Inc.
www.cj.com
Offers customized affiliate marketing programs and "fully-managed and integrated, comprehensive search engine marketing solutions."

LinkShare Corporation
www.linkshare.com
Popular network that optimizes management of your affiliate program. Provides search advantages, program news, and event information.

GRAPHIC DESIGN AND OTHER FREELANCERS

Guru
www.guru.com
Website states that Guru is "the world's largest online marketplace for freelance talent." Offers free service for employers to find top freelance and contract talent locally, nationally, or globally.

smarterwork
www.smarterwork.com
Smarterwork "specializes in bringing clients and qualified service providers together" for short-, medium-, or long-term projects.

Elance, Inc.
www.elance.com
Online workplace for small businesses to find, and hire, freelance people on-demand.

SOCIAL MEDIA MARKETING

del.icio.us
http://del.icio.us
Everything you need to know about social bookmarking and blogrolling in one place.

Last.fm Ltd.
www.last.fm
Tracks what you listen to, and gives you access to your favorite music.

CREATE A COMMUNITY OF USERS THROUGH AN OFF-SITE SOCIAL NETWORK.

Ning
www.ning.com
Ning "powers the largest number of social networks on the Internet." Offers social networking features that are "infinitely customizable to meet your unique needs" through a platform.

Facebook
www.facebook.com
Connect with people through this "social utility."

MySpace
www.myspace.com
Offers e-mail, a forum, communities, videos, and blog space internationally.

LinkedIn Corporation
www.linkedin.com
Focus is professional networking. Mission is "to help you be more effective in your daily work, and open doors to opportunities using the professional relationships you already have."

BROADEN YOUR NETWORK WITH ON-SITE INSTALLATION TOOLS.

Drupal
http://drupal.org
This software provides an open source content management platform that is used to support a variety of websites ranging from large community-driven sites to personal weblogs.

BoonEx
Shark
www.boonex.com/products/shark
Increase your revenue and the popularity of your community with Shark's enterprise community platform.

ONEsite, Inc.
www.onesite.com
Social network platform, offering cross-domain networking and an interactive media player.

Ramius Corporation
CommunityZero
www.communityzero.com/index.jsp
An interactive website that has "access to a suite of powerful tools that enable a group to become effectively organized, share knowledge, and communicate."

Community Server
http://communityserver.org
Community Server is a social networking platform "built to help you communicate more effectively with your customers." Allows you to participate in the "conversations that your customers are already having about your products or services."

CREATE A PRESENCE IN VIRTUAL WORLDS.

Second Life
http://secondlife.com
Do you have an avatar? You know, a persona in the virtual world. If not, check out this website and create your avatar to experience this 3-D online digital world.

CREATE A UNIQUE OR CONTROVERSIAL STORY, AND SUBMIT IT FOR EXPOSURE.

Digg, Inc.
http://digg.com
Discover and share content from anywhere on the web and through various digital mediums. Digg prides itself on not using editors, so it provides "a place where people can collectively determine the value of content." Digg is an alternative way for people to consume information online.

AOL, LLC
Netscape
http://netscape.aol.com
Discover news about anything and everything—even things that aren't really news.

CLAIM YOUR BLOG, AND BUILD UP ITS REPUTATION. EXCHANGE BLOGROLL LINKS WITH OTHER RELATED BLOGGERS. USE BLOGGING TOOLS TO TRACK SUBSCRIBERS AND DISTRIBUTE BLOG POSTS AUTOMATICALLY AS E-MAIL.

Technorati, Inc.
http://technorati.com
According to Technorati's website, it tracks 112.8 million blogs and more than 250 million pieces of tagged social media.

Blogger
www.blogger.com/start
Create your own blog here for free. Just choose a template, and get started.

WordPress
http://wordpress.org
Download and install a software script without paying anyone a license fee. WordPress is a "semantic personal publishing platform with a focus on aesthetics, web standards, and usability."

Six Apart
TypePad
www.typepad.com
For businesses and individuals, TypePad offers customizable designs and tools to manage blog conversations. Allows your blog to "live on your domain name," automatically supporting feeds, podcasting, and videocasting.

FeedBurner, Inc.
www.feedburner.com/fb/a/home
Looking for a blog advertising network? FeedBurner provides media distribution and audience engagement services for blogs and RSS feeds. Offers tutorials to get you started.

MyBlogLog
www.mybloglog.com
Connect with fellow readers, obtain "widgets," and gain reader insights here.

Goodreads
www.goodreads.com
Track what the blogger is currently reading at this book recommendation website. Goodreads' mission is "to improve the process of reading and learning throughout the world."

Twitter, Inc.
http://twitter.com
Track what the blogger is currently doing from this website. Twitter is a social networking and microblogging service that utilizes instant messaging and a web interface.

ADD INFORMATION ABOUT YOUR COMPANY TO THE INTERNET. (SEE ALSO: ZOOM INFORMATION, INC., LISTED ABOVE UNDER RESOURCES HEADING "MARKET INFORMATION.")

Squidoo, LLC
www.squidoo.com
Want to share your knowledge and passion with the world? Start your own page about anything! After all, everyone is an expert on something.

Wikipedia
http://wikipedia.org
Wikipedia is the free online encyclopedia offered in hundreds of languages. It has compiled information on more than seven million topics.

CREATE INTERESTING VIDEOS SHOWING WHAT YOU DO, AND POST THEM ON VIDEO SHARING SITES.

YouTube, LLC
www.youtube.com
This website needs no formal introduction. "Go to YouTube and Broadcast Yourself."

Metacafe, Inc.
www.metacafe.com
Post a video, and view videos online from people all over the world.

Flickr
www.flickr.com
Online photo management and sharing application.

RockYou
www.rockyou.com
Offers photo slideshows with music, videos, themes, movie posters, and more.

CREATE AND DISTRIBUTE PODCASTS.

Apple, Inc.
iTunes
www.iTunes.com
Turn whatever suits you into a digital file with iTunes.

SonicMountain
Odeo
http://odeo.com/
Audio channels, podcasts, music, and so much more is found when you listen, download, or subscribe to Odeo for free.

INCORPORATE YOUR BUSINESS

BizFilings
www.incorporating.com
Helps entrepreneurs and small business owners learn about incorporation and its benefits. BizFilings can help you "easily and affordably undertake this important business step without sacrificing quality."

PAY YOUR TAXES

Internal Revenue Service (IRS)
www.irs.gov/pub/irs-pdf/f2553.pdf
Have you decided to file your business as an S-Corporation? If so, follow this link to Form 2553 and request certain tax advantages for your small business from the federal government.

SOFTWARE FOR KEEPING TRACK OF YOUR FINANCES

Intuit, Inc.
QuickBooks
http://quickbooks.intuit.com

Quicken
http://quicken.intuit.com
Accounting software programs to help your business succeed and get your personal finances organized.

Microsoft Corporation
Microsoft Money
www.microsoft.com/money/default.mspx
Now known as Microsoft Money Plus, these accounting software programs enable you to become a financial expert.

Millionaire Blueprints Teen *neither endorses nor recommends any of the companies listed as resources. Resources are intended as a starting point for your research.*

PAY-PER-CLICK (PPC) ADVERTISING

This affordable form of Internet advertising lets you create a short advertisement of around ten to fifteen words that appears with a link to your website, alongside the results displayed in search engines. You only pay for your advertisement to appear when someone clicks through to your website.

PPC fees range from five cents to one-hundred dollars. You can set a daily budget. For example, you might pay ten cents for every click, but not more than ten dollars per day.

You simply create your advertisement, specify key search words that will trigger your advertisement to appear, and select languages and geographical regions. Once you give your billing information, your ad is activated within minutes. You can change your PPC fees and budget any time. Start low, and see what happens.

SO, YOU WANT TO WRITE AN E-BOOK?

IT'S EASIER THAN YOU THINK!

Are you an expert on a particular subject? Do you know everything there is to know about gardening, trading stocks, or world peace? Then why not share your expertise by creating an e-book? E-books are one of the most profitable online businesses today! As a matter of fact, an e-book can be written for very little cost, and, in most cases, brings in almost 100 percent profit. So, what exactly is an e-book? It is a digital version of a book.

You can write an e-book on just about anything from catalogs and user manuals, to novels and how-to guides. You can use any word processor. Perhaps the most popular is Microsoft Word (**www.microsoft.com**), but dependable alternatives include WordPerfect (**www.corel.com**) and OpenOffice (**www.openoffice.org**), with the latter being available for free. Writing your e-book doesn't have to be difficult; find out who your target audience is, and write accordingly. Write a synopsis first—one or more pages of text summarizing what your book is about. Then, using the synopsis as your guide, break the book into chapters, with each chapter touching on a certain facet of the book. The book should be well organized and allow your readers to locate information quickly and easily. Be sure to keep it readable and focused on the topic at hand.

Once written, you'll want to convert your e-book into a format that your readers can easily download and read. HTML and Adobe's PDF format are two of the more popular file formats that will allow your e-book to be viewed on everything from desktop and laptop computers, to Palms, pocket PCs, and smart phones.

An HTML-formatted book is an e-book that looks and feels exactly like a website. Most word processors have a "Save as HTML" feature that will easily convert your book into HTML.

The PDF format is probably the most versatile file type for e-book distribution. PDF files retain all the original file's formatting and layout. They can be attached to e-mails, downloaded from the Internet, posted on websites, and burned to CDs. With the proper plug-in, they can also be viewed within your browser. There are many PDF conversion programs on the market today. Adobe Acrobat (**www.adobe.com**) is the original PDF creation program, and it does an excellent job. However, low-cost alternatives by Easy PDF Creator (**www.pdfdesk.com**) and PDF Online (**www.pdfonline.com**) help bring the cost of creating a PDF file down to a very affordable level.

To prevent unauthorized alteration and duplication of your e-book, you may want to look into an e-book compiler such as Activ E-Book Compiler (**www.ebookcompiler.com**) or eBookGold software (**www.ebookgold.com**). An e-book compiler is a software program that can convert your word processing file into a stand-alone, executable format. A good e-book compiler will securely lock your file and allow access to customers who purchase a legitimate unlock code. Most e-book compilers are very affordable—between $30 to $100—and generally pay for themselves with less instances of fraud and with more e-book sales.

Before you sell your e-book, consider copyrighting your work. Copyrighting protects your e-book from being copied and claimed by someone else. Copyrighting also secures your rights in court, should you have to defend your work. For more information on copyrighting your work, visit the Library of Congress's U.S. Copyright Office at

www.loc.gov/copyright, or register with them through Click & Copyright at **www.clickandcopyright.com**. It's fast, easy, and well worth the $45 basic registration fee or the $35 electronic filing fee. (These costs were updated by the U.S. Copyright Office on July 1, 2007.)

Once you've copyrighted your e-book, you'll need a place to sell it and a way to accept payment. Many websites, such as eBookMall Publishing Center (**www.ebookmall-publishing.com**) and BookSurge (**www.booksurge.com**), will list your book for sale, and will handle all the marketing and selling details. Check their guidelines closely to understand exactly how you're getting paid. Some charge very high commission rates.

If you have the technical knowledge, or the resources to hire a web designer, you can set up your own website to market and sell your e-book. You'll need an electronic shopping cart system and a credit card processor to manage sales.

A shopping cart system allows your customers to view and select an e-book from a catalog of books. Companies like Volusion (**www.volusion.com**) and Web Genie Software (**www.webgenie.com**) offer affordable shopping cart solutions.

A credit card processor manages credit card transactions on your website. It ensures that the charge is legitimate and then transfers the funds to your merchant account. ClickBank (**www.clickbank.com**) and PayPal (**www.paypal.com**) offer credit card processing services for a nominal per-transaction fee. They're safe, secure, and accept most popular payment methods.

With a little time and effort, writing and marketing an e-book can be rewarding and profitable. So, turn on your computer and get to work on that e-book you've always wanted to write. You may just be the next bestselling e-book author on the web!

THE FIFTEEN-STEP PROCESS TO RAISING VENTURE CAPITAL

BY RYAN P. ALLIS

The process of raising venture funding generally follows a progression from introduction, to presentation, to term sheet, to due diligence, to closing. Depending on which stage you're in—along with your experience, reputation, and connections—some of these steps may be different or not applicable. The first step to gaining early-stage investments for your business is finding venture capitalists. In other words, this means finding professional investors to give you start-up money.

THE INTRODUCTION

You are introduced to a firm through a former entrepreneur that the firm has invested in through an investor they've worked with in the past, through a trusted attorney they know, or at a venture conference.

THE INITIAL REVIEW

An associate at the firm reviews your executive summary and gives a cursory look at your full plan and projections. If interested, the associate schedules a call with you. It helps if you already have existing revenue or have had a previous successful venture.

THE FIRST CALL

You speak with the associate by phone about what you are doing.

THE PARTNER DISCUSSION

If the associate likes what you are doing, he or she speaks to a partner at the firm about the opportunity.

THE FIRST MEETING

If you can get the interest of a partner, he or she will initiate a meeting either at their office or at yours (if you have one) depending on their level of interest and your location. During this first meeting, you will generally discuss the following about your venture:

• Background and experience
• Team makeup
• Competition
• Product differentiation
• Market size
• Funding needs

THE VALUATION DISCUSSION

After the first meeting, if the partner remains interested, he or she may attempt to feel you out for the target valuation you are seeking. He or she may also choose not to discuss valuation, and simply make an offer with the term sheet. If you are in a position of strength, you may wish to discuss valuation upfront yourself, so you don't waste time. Be prepared with revenue multiples from both public companies that are similar to yours and with private comparables. Depending on many factors (team, technology, industry stage, revenue growth, market size), one can expect to be able to raise funds at two to ten times the revenues from the trailing twelve months, or one to four times the projected revenues from the next twelve months. If you don't have any revenues yet, the valuation will be whatever you can negotiate with an investor—based upon your experience and any intellectual property you have. At the end of the day, the market valuation for your company is what an investor is willing to pay. As such, it is important to have multiple firms competing to invest in your venture, if possible. Depending on the stage of your company, you may be able to raise funds at a 30-percent to 60-percent discount off the public market trailing or forward revenue comparables.

THE PARTNER PRESENTATION

If you can come to a general valuation range that you are both comfortable with, the partner may invite you to present in person or via videoconference to their full partner team. Prepare well, and give a knockout presentation. Invest in a graphic designer to make your presentation look nice. Go heavy on actual examples of customer use and light on complex slides. A short product demonstration video, or customer video interview within the presentation, works well. Don't let any slide have more than five bullet points or contain more than fifty words. Your presentation is likely to be between fifteen and sixty minutes.

THE INITIAL DUE DILIGENCE

If the partners like the deal after the presentation to the full partner team, they may ask for some additional due diligence items—such as your full financials—and want to speak with other members of your team and some of your customers.

THE TERM SHEET

If all goes well during the initial due diligence phase, the venture firm may provide you with a term sheet. A term sheet is generally around two to eight pages, and is an indication of interest in investing in you. With a term sheet, the investment firm attempts to create agreement around the general terms of the deal before the lawyers create the more extensive twenty- to forty-page investment agreement document. Depending on the dollar amount, you will sometimes raise money from multiple firms at once in a syndicate deal. If this is the case, one firm will likely lead the deal and the other firm(s) will agree to the same term sheet. Often, the first interested firm will be able to bring syndicate partners to the table. However, sometimes you may need to find them yourself.

THE ATTORNEY REVIEW

Once you receive a term sheet, have your attorney review it right away and provide feedback before you discuss it with the investment firm.

THE TERM SHEET NEGOTIATION

Once you have reviewed the term sheet with your attorney, have a follow-up conversation with the partner or associate you are dealing with to negotiate the term sheet. Make sure you know which terms are the most important to you going into any negotiation (generally the valuation, option pool size, liquidation preference, participation preferred, founder revesting, and preferred stock veto rights). You may wish to have your attorney or your chief financial officer (CFO), if you have one, negotiate the finer points directly with the firm's attorney. At this point, it is critical to have a top-tier venture attorney on your side. These attorneys generally bill between $250 and $500 per hour, depending on their experience and on the market. Your negotiating power will be based upon the following:

- How much you need the money
- The reputation of the firm
- Your reputation as an entrepreneur
- Any past successes you've had
- Your experience
- The quality of your management team
- The members of your advisory panel
- The size of your addressable market
- Your market timing
- The quality of your technology
    and Internet protocol (IP)
- Your ability to walk away
- Whether you have other competing term sheets

Know that it is generally taboo to provide specifics to one firm about another firm's term sheet, but you can often provide generalities or refer to wanting to have a competitive process in order to have more power in negotiating the term sheet. Do not sign the term sheet until you have negotiated it to your satisfaction, and until your attorney approves the signing. Once you sign a term sheet, it is very difficult to negotiate any changes in the final document. If you can create a parallel process and receive multiple term sheets, you will have more power.

It will often take three or four negotiation interactions to put a term sheet together that makes both sides happy. It can take a lot of time (and a few thousand dollars in attorney fees) to effectively accomplish this, and it may be impossible without the right experience and revenues. It is often difficult to create a truly competitive process during the seed round, but with substantial annual revenues, great technology, and rapid growth, accomplishing a competitive round is more likely. While it can traditionally take six to eight weeks after the first meeting to get a term sheet from a venture firm, once you have an existing term sheet, you may be able to get competing term sheets in as little as one to two weeks. Group mentality does at times take hold, causing the valuation to be bid up with multiple players in the deal and causing some of the secondary terms to be softened. At some point, it can be unhealthy to push the valuation up. The best firms for you to work with are not always the highest bidders.

THE TERM SHEET SIGNING

Agree to the general terms of the deal. Either digitally sign the term sheet, or sign in person.

THE FULL DUE DILIGENCE

Once you sign the term sheet, a more extensive due diligence list will be provided to you. This list may include items such as:

- Detailed sales pipeline
- Revenue by customer type
- Detailed operational plan and budget
- Full business plan
- Hiring plan
- Detailed revenue assumptions
- Audited financial statements
- Bank reconciliation detail
- Product pricing list
- Detailed product road map
- Customer, employee, insurance, and lease contracts
- Relevant white papers (persuasive authoritative reports)
- Pertinent analyst coverage
- Details on information technology (IT) infrastructure

- Current partner list
- Lead generation processes
- Customer satisfaction survey
- Customer reference list
- Details on intellectual property
- Current capitalization chart with options detail
- Organizational chart
- Salary and bonus structure for company
- Employee turnover
- Management background checks
- Competitive analysis
- Expected acquirers
- Past board meeting minutes

THE FINAL INVESTMENT DOCUMENTS

Once this due diligence is complete, if all goes well, you will receive the final investment documents from the investment firm's lawyers. Have your attorney review them closely, and negotiate any needed changes. Pay especially close attention to any representations and warranties you are making, both as an officer of the company and on a personal basis. The final investment documents generally include the following:

- Share purchase agreement
- Investor rights agreement
- Right of first refusal and co-sale agreement
- Voting agreement

THE DEAL SIGNING

Provide your company bank account information, close the deal, watch the funds go into your account, breathe a sigh of relief, send out the press release, welcome your new

investor(s) and board member(s) to the team with a cele-
bration open house, exchange company particulars, and
send thank-you cards. Then, get going on growing revenue.

As you can see, the process can be lengthy, especially if
you are dealing with multiple firms and are trying to create
a competitive round. Even if a firm is not interested, try to
build a relationship for the future.

THE KEY TERMS OF A VENTURE TERM SHEET

THE OFFERING

Closing Dates: *The target date for the close of the deal.*
Investors: *Which firm(s) will invest in the deal.*
Amount Raised: *How much money you are investing.*
Pre-Money Valuation: *The agreed-upon value of your
company before the investment.*
Post-Money Valuation: *The value of your company after
the investment. This is equal to the pre-money valuation plus
the investment amount.*
Capitalization: *The company's current shareholder list
with the number of shares and options of each shareholder.*
Use of Proceeds: *How the investment money is to be used.*

THE CHARTER

Dividends: *The process by which dividends will be distrib-
uted to shareholders. Dividend distribution generally occurs at
the discretion of the board. This section also includes the interest rate at which the investment funds will grow each year, on
either a cumulative or noncumulative basis. Try to negotiate
out any interest, or at least request no interest in the case of a
successful exit.*
Liquidation Preference: *The right for the investor(s) to
receive their money out first in a liquidity event before
payment is made to common shareholders.*

Voting Rights: Covers the rights of the investor(s) to vote on certain items materially affecting the company.

Protective Provisions: Describes what company changes need to be approved by the investor(s).

Anti-Dilution Provisions: The right of the investor(s) to be protected from dilution in the event that stock is ever sold at a price less than the current round (called a down-round). The broad-based weighted average is the method of calculating dilution that is most company friendly.

Mandatory Conversion: Describes the conditions and process by which the preferred shares convert into common shares.

Optional Conversion: The right of the investor(s) to convert their preferred shares into common shares at any point in time.

Redemption Rights: The right of the investor(s) to get their money back if they choose to after a period of time—generally, after five years. This is a rarely used provision, but be careful with it nonetheless.

THE STOCK PURCHASE AGREEMENT

Representations and Warranties: Must be true and accurate for the investment to take place.

Conditions to Closing: A general description of the due diligence area to be looked at prior to closing.

Counsel and Expenses: Covers the maximum amount of money due the attorneys to close the deal. Generally, between $10,000 and $30,000, depending on the complexity of the deal. The company will usually pay this out of the investment amount.

THE INVESTOR RIGHTS AGREEMENT

Registration Rights: Refers to the rights of the investor(s) to register their shares during a public offering.

Information and Inspection Rights: The rights of the investor(s) to receive information about the company.

Board Matters/Size: The composition of the board of directors following the deal. Do your best to ensure that there are more company representatives than investor representatives. You effectively lose control of the company if this is not the case. You may wish for your board to be your chief executive officer (CEO), chairman, or chief financial officer (CFO), and one investor. Or you may want to expand to five members and have your CEO, CFO, chairman, and two investor representatives.

Drag-Along: The right of the board and preferred shareholders to ensure that all stockholders will agree to sign if the board and majority of the preferred stockholders agree to sell.

Right of First Refusal: The right of the company and/or the investor(s) to purchase any shares that any shareholder chooses to sell.

THE OTHER MATTERS

Bank Debt: Any related line-of-credit that the investor(s) expressly approve.

Employment Matters: A condition of closing requiring all employees to have employment contracts and noncompete agreements.

No Shop/Confidentiality: An agreement not to tell anyone outside of company shareholders, the board of directors, and your attorney about the terms of the deal, or to seek other term sheets during a period of usually thirty to forty-five days while the deal is being closed.

Binding/Nonbinding Provisions: Any obligations that

the term sheet will legally bind the parties to, whether or not the deal is executed, such as paying the legal fees of the investor(s).

Expiration: *The date after which the term sheet offer is no longer valid. Don't let this date cause you to sign the term sheet before you are ready.*

THE TWELVE TIPS FOR ANYONE ATTEMPTING TO RAISE VENTURE CAPITAL

It takes time to learn about the many components of a term sheet. It can be very valuable to have an attorney or CFO advise you through the process. At the end of the day, don't sign the term sheet until you are fully comfortable with it and understand the provisions within.

TIP 1

Get introduced through an entrepreneur or an attorney to a venture capitalist (VC) they have worked with in the past. A good law firm can be very valuable for investor introductions—if you can convince them that your business would be a good investment.

TIP 2

Talk to multiple firms at once. Create a competitive process, and seek multiple term sheets if you are able.

TIP 3

Read up on term sheet terminology, and have a good understanding of this before you start talking to investors. The key terms are pre-money valuation, liquidation preference, participation, share revesting (revert shares back to former owner), dividends, board size, and protective provisions (veto controls).

TIP 4

Be upfront about the general terms. You are seeking to save time for yourself and for the investor.

TIP 5

Know that the pre-money valuation is only one of the important terms.

TIP 6

Become involved with organizations in your community that can connect you to other entrepreneurs who have raised venture capital before, and then have lunch with those entrepreneurs.

TIP 7

Realize that it will probably take at least nine months to raise money from start to finish your first time out.

TIP 8

Realize that, until you have at least $1 million in annual revenue, it may be difficult to get most VCs interested, unless you have had prior successes or have really unique technology.

TIP 9

Know that it may take six months of sustained product and revenue progress after your first meeting before a VC will consider your deal seriously.

TIP 10

Know how much money you are trying to raise before you begin discussions.

TIP 11

Know that it may be easier to seek angel funding or debt funding instead of venture capital early on in the process. Angel funding is from an investor who has experience and interest relevant to your company's mission. Debt funding is money given contingent upon repayment of its principal interest.

TIP 12

Know that once you sign a term sheet, it will be at least thirty days—and can be up to ninety days—before you actually close on the funds.

THE RESOURCES

FundingPost
www.fundingpost.com
Website offers a wide assortment of information, including a glossary of venture capital terms and details on venture conferences.

Millionaire Blueprints Teen *neither endorses nor recommends any of the companies listed as resources. Resources are intended as a starting point for your research.*

CHAPTER 3

Michael
SIMMONS
and
Sheena
LINDAHL

Extreme Entrepreneur Team rolls big.

BUSINESS NAME(S):
Extreme Entrepreneurship Education Corporation, LLC (EEEC)

BUSINESS TYPE(S):
Entrepreneurship Motivation and Skills

LOCATION:
New York, NY

M*ichael Simmons has been creating opportunities for success since he was sixteen years old. Without business experience, but with a great idea and a huge amount of confidence, he landed his first client in his first meeting. Simmons cofounded his first business, Princeton WebSolutions (PWS), when he was just sixteen. PWS was later rated the number one youth-run web development company in the nation by* YoungBiz *magazine. In addition, Simmons has been the winner of three Entrepreneur of the Year Awards from the National Foundation for Teaching Entrepreneurship (NFTE), Fleet, and the National Coalition for Empowering Youth Entrepreneurs.*

This early success laid the groundwork for what would become his first book, The Student Success Manifesto. *The book led to speaking engagements, which led to the Extreme Entrepreneurship Tour (EET). Now Simmons and his partner and coauthor, Sheena Lindahl, are crossing the country in a giant recreational vehicle (RV) to share their message with students everywhere. They have been keynote speakers on the topics of student success and youth entrepreneurship at events and conferences from Washington state to Washington, D.C.*

These 2005 graduates of New York University (NYU) are authors, teachers, speakers, and award-winning entrepreneurs, and they are able to deliver a unique perspective that connects with audiences. Recently, the team of Simmons and Lindahl was named by BusinessWeek *magazine as one of its "Top Twenty-five Entrepreneurs Under Twenty-five."*

Millionaire Blueprints Teen *caught up with Simmons recently, and he opened up about the steps he took that have put him on the road to success, literally, in a big old RV.*

GETTING INTO THEIR BUSINESS

Tell us about your first business venture.

In 1998, I had a web development company with Cal Newport. We created a basic website. In high school, we used SCORE.org to get a lot of answers to our questions.

How much did it cost to get started?

At the time, the Internet was more expensive, so we spent seventy dollars on a domain name and twenty dollars per month in webhosting. Within a month, we were found on Yahoo! by potential customers.

What was the name of your company, and why?

Originally, it was Princeton Internet Solutions. The first client found us when they searched for "Princeton" and "web development" on Yahoo.com. We named it that because we were fifteen minutes from Princeton, and we thought it sounded prestigious. After our first meeting, we changed it to Princeton Web Solutions because the client pointed out that our acronym spelled out PIS. This was not good.

Did they know that you were teenagers before you showed up for the meeting?

They had no idea we were kids. The meeting went well, but at the end they asked, "How old are you?" We were trying to hide our age, but the guy saw it as an advantage. They loved it that we were "young techie people."

How did you manage school and business ownership?

An outsourcing company in India e-mailed us, and we decided to try them out. They had a team of people, a great website, and looked legitimate. Ultimately, it was a great decision.

How long did that business last?

It lasted for three years—until the dot-com bust. All the companies went out of business, so they stopped needing our services. The partnership broke up when we went to different colleges. I went to NYU School of Business. He went to Dartmouth College. Our experience together formed a foundation for the success each of us enjoyed.

What kind of success has your old partner garnered?

Cal Newport published two books, *How to Become a Straight-A Student* and *How to Win at College*. He graduated with honors as a member of the

Phi Beta Kappa Society from Dartmouth College in 2004, and is currently a computer science Ph.D. candidate at the Massachusetts Institute of Technology (MIT). You can find him through his website at **www.calnewport.com**.

So, what happened once you went to college?

I met my business partner, Sheena Lindahl (who soon became my girl-friend, and, eventually, my wife), during orientation at NYU. We were both already thinking entrepreneurially. NYU tuition is $35,000 a year. She paid her tuition at NYU herself by learning how loans and credit cards worked. She worked with the America Reads program in classrooms and was pro-moted quickly, making an impressive forty dollars per hour.

How did you get your book published?

We self-published *The Student Success Manifesto*. And Sheena started writing its companion workbook. The goal was to help people create a strategic life plan like they would create a business plan.

What steps did you take to self-publish?

We found an editor, Tony Towle, through our mentor, Steve Mariotti, who is president and founder of The National Foundation for Teaching Entrepreneurship (NFTE). I designed the cover. We used a photo by pho-tographer Bob Handelman (**www.bobhandelman.com**) that had been used in *NYU Magazine*. We used Microsoft Word to lay it out, which is not the industry standard, but it got the job done.

How did you get an International Standard Book Number (ISBN)?

We searched **www.ISBN.org** for all of our information. Also, you can get a universal product code (UPC) for eighty-nine dollars at **www.UPCcode.net**.

How did you get involved in speaking at colleges?

I would speak at conferences with teachers and administrators. I would e-mail the organizer or use any connections I might have to get in. Plus, I would send the book, which helped give us credibility.

How did you know where to try to get in to speak?

By searching for conferences. You should look for associations that bring the industry and industry practitioners together. Use the keyword "association" to do your Internet search. If you want to speak about fashion, you search "national fashion conference." We searched "entrepeneurship education conference." Speaking at conferences with educators led to inroads for campus visits.

What is the name of your current business?

It's Extreme Entrepreneurship Education Corporation, LLC (EEEC). The Extreme Entrepreneurship Tour is one of our products. The three main elements include: the Extreme Entrepreneurship Tour, our new accountability website (**www.journeypage.com**), and our merchandise—the book and a product called Tour-in-a-Box.

Why did you start your Extreme Entrepreneurship Road Tour?

We started getting invited to do more speaking engagements, so we decided to take it on the road. I think we got so many opportunities because we're young and we could provide a youthful perspective. For the road tour, we had the idea to bring in other student speakers as well.

What happens on the road tour?

The Extreme Entrepreneurship Tour brings the country's top young entrepreneurs to college campuses to deliver keynotes and half-day educational programs. The tour focuses on two themes: success and leadership, and entrepreneurship. We do a four-hour event with the keynote speaker, workshops, panels, and a social networking event. You can bring it to your school by e-mailing Sheena at: sheena@extremetour.org, or by calling 800-930-8021.

How many schools have you been to so far?

We have gone to more than 100 schools. Our title sponsor is Venture Port, but we have also partnered with Inc.com, Advantage Networks, Operation Enterprise, Collegiate Entrepreneurs Organization, and many more.

How do people sign up for one of your events?

Students register through their schools, or we have an RSVP (please reply) option on our website. Anyone in the area can attend if they register. They don't have to be students of the college. If the school promotes it, then more people come.

THE MARKETING

Who does the marketing for the Extreme Entrepreneurship Tour?

We leave marketing up to the schools. We don't give them printed materials. We let them use their own printers, and they can customize them with their own logos. They know their market, so they know what works. We provide resources, templates, and high-resolution files. It's all very turnkey for the schools.

Tell us about the bus on your website. Did you buy the RV?

It's a forty-foot RV, and yes, we own it. We rent a facility in New Jersey where we keep it parked for about $150 a month. We searched and found it online. We wrapped it, so it would be good for advertising, too. Because it's an RV, it doesn't require a special license to drive.

THE INTERNET

What is JourneyPage.com?

It is our interactive website, which inspires people to take action. It offers accountability and coaching. It also connects people through conference calls, so they can hold each other accountable throughout the day.

How do you charge for this service?

We charge a monthly fee for people to be on calls. Conference calls are every morning at 6:52 and at 8:52. They say what they will do and what they will get done that day. It's called Power Hour. Within the first three months, we grew exponentially. We wanted to promote it with the road tour.

Who hosts the site?

LunarPages.com hosts the website. It costs about $100 per month. We use **www.FreeConferenceCalls.com**, which allows us to do the conference calls for free.

How many people subscribe to the quarterly newsletter from your ExtremeE.org website?

About 5,000 people subscribe. (**NOTE:** *Millionaire Blueprints Teen* is one of the subscribers. When we saw this site, we had to get in the loop!)

How would someone set up an e-newsletter?

We use iContact.com. And we send out a DreamER story every quarter. These are dreams that went to the "emergency room" and survived. They are stories about situations that were not going well, but where the businesses bounced back. In other words, they survived.

THE LEGAL

What type of legal advice did you receive to prepare to launch your business?

We incorporated as a limited liability company (LLC), and we trademarked the name Extreme Entrepreneurship with a lawyer from Friedman Kaplan Seiler & Adelman LLP (**www.fkslaw.com**). They handle all of our legal affairs. We have also benefited from pro bono legal advice from Liza Vertinski, who now works at Emory University as an assistant professor of law specializing in intellectual property law.

THE MONEY

What kinds of costs were involved, specifically, with the start up of your company?

The costs were minimal. We printed brochures, and we paid to travel to conferences. Fortunately, we were accepted into the Stern Incubator at my school, NYU. The Stern Incubator is an educational and experiential program of NYU Stern and the Berkley Center for Entrepreneurial Studies (BCES).

What is an incubator?

An incubator gives student-led teams of entrepreneurs a unique way to develop their business concepts. You get work space, infrastructure (such as access to high-speed Internet connections, computers, cubicles, conference rooms, and telephones), and other business essentials to facilitate the process of launching your businesses into the real world. We got four hours of free consulting from the program's accountant, plus legal and strategy advice. MBA students also helped us. People should investigate incubators. Their school might have one. You can do a Google search to find one near you.

What about your book?

We went to Lightening Source to find a print-on-demand publisher. You can find all kinds of publishers listed at **www.lighteningsource.com**. We used a print broker. We paid four dollars and eight cents for each book when we ordered several hundred. When we ordered 5,000, they were one dollar and eighty-three cents each. The rest was profit. We sell at our Extreme Entrepreneurship Tours (EET), from our website, and it's also available on Amazon.com.

What other ways do you sell your book?

The best way to sell it is through bulk purchases—through organizations like the NFTE. My mentor wrote the foreword, so that was helpful. My first sales were to people who already knew me and my track record.

What type of merchandise do you sell?

We sell my book, *The Student Success Manifesto* and a Tour-in-a-Box package, which includes tapes and materials from our road tour for anyone who might want to take what they've heard at the EET home with them.

The Extreme Entrepreneur team has proven to be a formidable force in the business world, as well as on college campuses across the nation. The message they deliver is so highly regarded, that corporate sponsors are lining up to join forces with them. The concept of teaching extreme entrepreneurship to students across the country continues to change lives and inspire people to go after their dreams. We can only hope that this stellar team decides to extend its road tour schedule into the future. Until then, keep an eye out for Simmons's second book (soon to be launched), All or Nothing, Now or Never.

Simmons and Lindahl are riding high on the wave of their success. And, these days, they're riding that wave in a forty-foot RV.

THE PLAN TO FOLLOW

STEP 1

Create a strategic life plan.

STEP 2

Participate in incubator programs.

NOTE: Simmons urges you to investigate incubators. Your school may have one. Just do a Google search, and find one near you.

STEP 3

Get legal and accounting advice.

NOTE: Ask your mentor to refer you to someone he or she uses.

STEP 4

Consider outsourcing to save money.

STEP 5

Use print-on-demand self-publishing services.

NOTE: Simmons says that the best way to sell your book is through bulk purchases from professional associations in your field of interest. He sold his book in bulk to the NFTE.

STEP 6

Go to industry conferences.

NOTE: Simmons advises you to look for associations that bring the industry and industry practitioners together. Use the keyword "association" to do your Internet search.

THE HIGHLIGHTS

- Hold yourself accountable by setting goals and meeting them.
- Let your life lessons become foundations for future success.
- If you want to publish your creation, consider self-publishing.
- Inspire others to take action, and motivate yourself in the process.
- Use your personal and professional contacts to network with others.

THE RESOURCES

Extreme Entrepreneurship Education Corporation, LLC (EEEC)
www.ExtremeE.org
Do you have an entrepreneurial mind-set? EEEC is a media and educational company helping college students plan, prioritize, and pursue their dreams. EEEC's books, online community, and speaking tours provide students with the tools and inspiration they need to launch their own businesses.

Extreme Entrepreneurship Tour (EET)
www.ExtremeTour.org
Business offers the EET college road tour that focuses on entrepreneurship and achieving dreams. Website offers purchase of the Tour-in-a-Box package and an online newsletter to keep you informed on possible new tour dates. You can bring it to your school by e-mailing Lindahl at:

sheena@extremetour.org, or by calling 800-930-8021.

JourneyPage
www.journeypage.com
Want to celebrate your victories and share your goals? Get in contact with life coaches, and participate in daily "get stuff done" group calls. Website also offers personal accountability tools. JourneyPage is part of the Extreme Entrepreneurship Education Corporation, LLC (EEEC).

Cal Newport
www.calnewport.com
Website includes this author's blog, selections from his articles, and excerpts from his books—all meant to "demystify college success."

Venture Port
www.ventureport.org
Website features links to resources and networks, a marketplace, a forum and a blog, videos, and event information.

Inc.com
www.inc.com
An all-encompassing resource for entrepreneurs.

Advantage Networks
http://goadvnet.com
Progressive programs and strategies for college, mobile, and sports marketing.

YoungBiz
www.youngbiz.com
Written for teens and by teens, YoungBiz has an online guide and a magazine dedicated to business, careers, investing, and entrepreneurship.

SCORE
www.SCORE.org
Website states it is "America's premier source of free and confidential small business advice for entrepreneurs."

BOOKS

Simmons, Michael. *The Student Success Manifesto: How to Create a Life of Passion, Purpose, and Prosperity.* New York: Extreme Entrepreneurship Education, LLC, 2003.

Newport, Cal. *How to Become a Straight-A Student: The Unconventional Strategies Real College Students Use to Score High While Studying Less.* New York: Broadway Books, 2006.

Newport, Cal. *How to Win at College: Surprising Secrets for Success from the Country's Top Students.* New York: Broadway Books, 2005.

LAWYERS

Friedman Kaplan Seiler & Adelman LLP
www.fkslaw.com
Represents clients in litigation and corporate transactions.

ASSOCIATIONS AND EDUCATIONAL PROGRAMS

National Business Incubation Association (NBIA)
www.nbia.org
20 East Circle Drive, Suite 37198
Athens, Ohio 45701-3571
740-593-4331
Fax: 740-593-1996
Website states NBIA is the "world's leading organization advancing business incubation and entrepreneurship." NBIA provides education, information, advocacy, and networking resources between professionals and early stage companies worldwide.

The National Foundation for Teaching Entrepreneurship (NFTE)
www.nfte.com
120 Wall Street, Twenty-Ninth Floor
New York, New York 10005
212-232-3333 or 800-FOR-NFTE
Helping youth from low-income communities find pathways to prosperity through entrepreneurship educational programs.

American Management Association
Operation Enterprise
www.amanet.org/oe
Operation Enterprise consists of management and leadership development programs for high school and college students. Its programs are
recommended for three semester hours of undergraduate credit by the
American Council on Education.

Collegiate Entrepreneurs' Organization
www.c-e-o.org
A global entrepreneurship network with 400 chapters and affiliated student organizations at colleges and universities.

The Stern Incubator
www.sternincubator.com
Just one of many college programs nationwide, the Stern Incubator helps
foster the development and growth of new business ideas.

Berkley Center for Entrepreneurial Studies (BCES)
http://w4.stern.nyu.edu/berkley
The BCES at New York University's Stern School of Business includes curriculum and research that explores and encourages entrepreneurship,
innovation, and new venture creation.

ACCOUNTANT

Janover Rubinroit, LLC
www.jrllc.com/info.html
805 Third Avenue, Tenth Floor
New York, New York 10022
212-792-6300
Fax: 212-792-6350
E-mail: info@jrllc.com
With seventy years of experience, this firm promises to serve your
accounting needs "the way we would wish to be served."

VEHICLE WRAPPING

AdWraps
www.ad-wraps.com
732-502-8300
Offers many types of product designs such as vehicle wraps, custom decals, wall graphics, window graphics, floor signs, banners, mega prints, and more.

EMC Outdoor
www.emcoutdoor.com
610-353-9300
Advertising for "any type of outdoor media in any market."

CONFERENCE CALLS

Free Conference
www.freeconferencecalls.com
Need to make conference calls? Check out all the services offered here.

E-NEWSLETTER

iContact
www.icontact.com
2635 Meridian Parkway
Durham, North Carolina 27713
866-803-9462
iContact is an on-demand e-mail marketing service that allows organizations of all sizes to automatically respond and distribute content to customers by creating, sending, and tracking e-mail newsletters, really simple syndication (RSS) feeds, and surveys.

SELF-PUBLISHING

Lightening Source
www.lighteningsource.com
Please note that this is a search engine. So, just enter "self-publishing" and scope out a self-publisher for your very own creation.

R. R. Bowker, LLC
www.isbn.org
Everything you need to know about ISBNs in one place. R. R. Bowker, LLC, is the official company with stewardship of the U.S. ISBN Agency.

Simply Barcodes
www.upccode.net
Purchase barcodes at this official seller of UPCs, making your products easy to scan when purchased.

PRINT BROKER

Book Market
www.bookmarket.com/printgp.htm
This link has a listing of print brokers to get you started in finding the one best for you.

BOOK OUTLET

Books Just Books.com
www.booksjustbooks.com
Provides book printing and self-publishing services, including editorial critiques and full copy editing services.

Amazon.com
www.amazon.com
Buy, sell, and shop online at this website that needs no introduction.

PHOTOGRAPHER

Bob Handelman Images
www.bobhandelman.com
2121 Durham Road
Madison, Connecticut 06443
212-352-9000
Fax: 203-241-5300
E-mail: info@bobhandelman.com
Photographic artist and visual storyteller.

RV SALES

rvSearch
www.rvsearch.com
Buy, sell, and find an RV dealer.

RV Net
www.rv.net
This link hosts a network of RV websites "dedicated to serving enthusiasts of the open road."

RV Trader
www.rvtrader.com
Online classifieds to find an RV.

WEBHOSTING

Add2Net, Inc.
Lunarpages Division
www.lunarpages.com
100 East La Habra Boulevard
La Habra, California 90631
714-521-8150
Offers a variety of customizable webhosting plans, and, coupled with the reputation of being the leading webhost in the industry, Lunarpages provides technicians, support, and hardware "to transform your online presence."

Millionaire Blueprints Teen neither endorses nor recommends any of the companies listed as resources. Resources are intended as a starting point for your research.

PROMOTING A SELF-PUBLISHED BOOK

"Self-publishing is not a fall-back position. It's my first choice," says Peter Bowerman, author of *The Well-Fed Writer* and its companion volume, *The Well-Fed Writer: Back For Seconds.* "No one will ever care about your book more than you do."

Big publishing houses rarely deliver the overnight success many authors dream about. Promoting a new book today requires a major commitment, regardless of the publishing method you choose. With self-publishing, you retain total control over marketing and keep more of the profits. In an interview with *Millionaire Blueprints Teen*, Bowerman shared some tricks of the self-publishing trade, and he showed us how the Internet can be an author's best friend.

A WORD ABOUT SELF-PUBLISHING

Self-publishing is a topic unto itself. In this article, we deal strictly with promoting your self-published book. For a host of articles full of advice and information on self-publishing, visit Writing World online at **www.writing-world.com**. That said, we do have one piece of advice for you in the self-publishing realm: Hire a professional publishing consultant. Bowerman says that he hired one the first time around, and the advice he received paid for itself many times over. One place you can find a professional publishing consultant is on the Publisher's Marketing Association (PMA) website (**www.pma-online.org**). And Bowerman, himself, now has such a wealth of knowledge and expertise in this area that he wrote a third book, *The Well-Fed Self-Publisher.*

"Self-publishing can be a black hole of time," Bowerman says. "To keep it from consuming you, hire a consultant who can steer you in the right direction."

For more tips on self-publishing, or to talk with Bowerman about becoming your own personal self-publishing mentor, visit his website at **www.wellfedwriter.com**.

MAKE A SUCCESSFUL START

Presentation is everything. If your book looks like it was self-published, the packaging can eclipse the writing. The cover, title, and printing all play a major role. Visit bookstores to look for covers and titles that catch your eye, and apply those concepts to your book. Hire a professional to design your cover. "Don't," Bowerman warns, "let your printer design your book cover." Put some thought into a title that is creative yet descriptive and that, in the case of a how-to book, is a promise. An example is *The Well-Fed Writer*.

Print your galleys (the prepublication version of your book) only in four-color, and make them look like the final version. Spiral bindings and folded and gathered (F&G) pages look amateurish, so use a professional finish for the spine. Bowerman recommends what is called "perfect binding." Choose paper and printing appropriate for the style of the book. Your book needs to look like it belongs in a bookstore if you want reviewers and readers to take it seriously.

BLURBS FOR THE COVER

There's nothing like a quote from a well-known personality to help sell a few copies. Look up related books on Amazon (**www.amazon.com**) by subject. Many include e-mail links to the authors. Alternatively, try anyone whose name will be recognized by your future readers. Contact them directly, through an editor, or by other writing resources. Ask if they will review your book and write a little blurb for your final cover. Be professional and respect their time, but aim high; the worst they can do is say, "No."

REVIEWS: THE KEY TO BOOK SALES

Bowerman recommends working your way up in layers, starting at the bottom and building success as you go. Approach the top layers only after building a reputation. Begin by identifying your target audience. Then search the web for associations, newsletters, and anyone who has a website catering to those groups.

For a listing of associations, try the following resources: The Marketing Resource Center (**www.marketingsource.com/ associations**), The Internet Public Library (IPL) (**www.ipl. org/div/aon**), and the Oxbridge Directory of Newsletters online at **www.oxbridge.com**. Go to MediaFinder (**www.mediafinder.com**) to research databases or just use keyword searches. You can also check the print version of *Gale's Directory* at a local library, or visit **http://gale. cengage.com** for more information.

Create a standard pitch letter with variations for different groups. Locate the "Contact Us" link on each website, and cut-and-paste your pitch letter into an e-mail. Your goal is to get them to read your book and post a review on their website. You can even offer to write the reviews for them. Bowerman discovered that many of his readers bought the book only after seeing several reviews. Therefore, get as many sites to post reviews as possible. Never send review copies to someone you have not contacted (either by e-mail or phone), or they'll likely end up in the trash. However, don't be shy about sending out review copies to anyone who asks. Once you've gotten several good reviews, make a list of the organizations, and note links to their websites. Use that list to approach bigger fish.

You're more likely to get noticed if you show that you're already establishing an audience.

Another avenue to try early on is book clubs. Try Writer's Digest Book Club (**www.writersdigestbookclub.com**) for writing books, and check the online version of Literary Market Place at **www.literarymarketplace.com** for a complete listing of book clubs, and much more. Once you've built up some reviews, approach the bigger clubs like Book-of-the-Month (**www.bomc.com**), Quality Paperback Book Club (**www.qpb.com**), and Doubleday Book Club (**www.doubledaybookclub.com**). Few things boost sales more than a well-placed "Selection of Book-of-the-Month Club," as Bowerman was fortunate to be able to do. Then, get on the databases from which big bookstores and libraries order.

MAGAZINE ARTICLES AS BOOK PROMOTIONS

Put together four or five interesting articles about your book. Make them of varying lengths from 250 to 1,500 words. Some might simply be excerpts from your book. Contact websites and publications whose audience matches yours, and ask to submit an article. As a rule, you won't be paid for the articles. But, with the final attribution paragraph explaining who you are, what you've written, and including your website address, it's wonderful free advertising. When someone requests one of these articles, all you have to do is send an e-mail.

YOUR WEBSITE: AN ABSOLUTE "MUST-HAVE"

Your book's website doesn't need to be twenty-five pages. You're selling one or two books, not 5,000 books. One reader told Bowerman how he set up a website in just a few hours for only $75 by using Go Daddy's (**www.godaddy.com**)

complete do-it-yourself site application. Use your website to showcase your book. Include reviews, an excerpt, or even a whole chapter. Make sure to provide detailed instructions on where, and how, to buy your book. Keep it simple with fast-loading pages, and consider using the same color scheme as your book cover. Insert a link to your website in every e-mail you send. Get the e-mail addresses of everyone you talk to in the process of promoting your book. Make a point of sending them a quick e-mail with a link to your website. They are less likely to visit it if you give them the address over the phone. Check out Bowerman's website for ideas (**www.wellfedwriter.com**). He's quick to note that his website has evolved dramatically over the years. So, starting small is fine.

WHEN TO MAKE YOURSELF "OFFICIAL"

Set your official publication date (OPD) three to six months after your bound book date (BBD), which is the day you receive final printed books. This gives you enough time to get the word out and start creating interest in your book. Some important magazines to get a review of your book placed in include *Library Journal* (**www.libraryjournal.com**), American Library Association's *Booklist* (**www.ala.org/booklist**), *Publishers Weekly* (**www.publishersweekly.com**), *ForeWord* (**www.forewordmagazine.com**), and *Kirkus Reviews* (**www.kirkusreviews.com**), just to name a few. Many reviewers only like to review up-and-coming books (meaning 90 to 120 days prior to the OPD), so be sure to leave plenty of time.

LIBRARY ACCESS: GETTING ON THE SHELVES

Busy librarians often order most of the books reviewed in their industry publications and rely on them to weed out the pack. Those include *Library Journal* and the others mentioned in the previous paragraph. The truth is that those publications only review about 10 percent to 15 percent of the books submitted to them. While your chances of getting reviewed are not high, it's worth a shot. If you make it in, you increase your credibility and your sales. What is Bowerman's advice about becoming one of the 10 percent to 15 percent? Write a good book, and remember that presentation is everything.

BOOKSTORES: CREATE DEMAND FIRST

Contrary to popular opinion, most people won't find your book while browsing the shelves. You need to create demand, and get people to look for it. When they don't find your book, they'll order it at the information desk. Get those reviews out there, and then get listed on one of the databases that bookstores can access such as Biblio Distribution (**www.bibliodistribution.com**), which is your door to Ingram Book Group (**www.ingrambook.com**), the huge wholesaler for the bookstores (known as "the trade"), or Baker & Taylor (**www.btol.com**), the wholesaler for the libraries. Check each website for links to something like "Publisher Requirements" or "Prospective Publishers" to determine what you need to do to qualify.

One fulfillment source (the physical shipment of your books to clients from the big buyers to the one-book buyer) that Bowerman recommends highly is BookMasters (**www.bookmasters.com**). They can do just about everything, except write the book for you. You can also visit the website of each major bookseller for instructions. Once bookstores start seeing demand for your book, they will begin to order copies on their own. The most important tip Bowerman shared with us regarding bookstores is this: If you push your book into the big chains without first creating demand, you may end up with a lot of returns, which average 25 percent to 30 percent or more, and has topped out in some nightmare scenarios as high as 60 percent! Often, the returned books are in poor condition and require a full refund. Using these strategies, Bowerman's return rate for 35,000 copies is less than 5 percent.

WHO SHOULD SELF-PUBLISH?

Any first-time author can self-publish. After that, it depends largely on the name you've made for yourself and on your book's category. Nonfiction—specifically how-to and other niche books—are best suited for self-publishing. On the other hand, fiction readers will browse the shelves in search of new titles. Once you've created a following with your first book, it can't hurt to consider a conventional publishing contract, but only if your potential audience is huge.

CONVENTIONAL PUBLISHING: THE SECOND CHOICE

A major publisher approached Bowerman in 2003, but he declined their offer. Now that he's gone through the process twice, he doesn't see an upside to going the conventional route. The money is less—often, a lot less—and you give up control of the process and sign away the rights to your creation. Depending on the market for your book, you probably won't make up in volume what you lose in per-book profits. On a twenty-dollar paperback, you might get to keep one dollar to two dollars per book with a conventional publisher, versus seven dollars to sixteen dollars (net profit) with self-publishing, depending on the distribution method you use.

When the publisher loses interest in marketing your book because something new comes along, you're stuck.

Some contracts specify that the rights revert to the author on a certain date, but you still have to wait. If your book deals with a current topic, the window of opportunity may close before you regain control.

TWO TIMES, A CHARM

When you're ready to publish your second book, you have two things going for you. One, you've been through it all before; and two, there's a little something Bowerman calls the "marketing boomerang." If you do enough marketing, you'll find reviews of your book in places that you've never contacted—or even heard of. The process begins to multiply on its own. When he began promoting his second book, Bowerman did an online search for all appearances of his name and book title. Due to the "boomerang" effect, the list had grown significantly. He contacted every group on the new list, asking if they would review his second book, too. His success rate was huge, since they had already reviewed the first one. Using these sources and a list of subscribers to his monthly e-zine (which he'd been publishing for thirty months at that point), Bowerman put out the word that his next book was on sale. During the first month, it was only available through his website (where his profit margins ran 80 percent to 85 percent), and he sold 450 copies. That's not a bad return for a few mass e-mails. Then he continued following the formula he created, and got it listed in the library journals and bookstore databases for wider distribution.

To date, Bowerman has sold more than 35,000 copies of his first book, and sales of his second and third books are chugging along nicely. Most conventional publishers think sales of 10,000 to 15,000 copies are good for niche books like his. With numbers like these, there's no reason to go the conventional route. Bowerman's last piece of advice is to always be looking for more contacts in your target communities. "A week doesn't go by that I'm not sending out two or three review copies," he says.

THE RESOURCES

Peter Bowerman
www.wellfedwriter.com
Self-publishing and commercial freelancing professional coach. Check out this website for Bowerman's books in e-book format. Learn what this expert has to offer you.

Bowerman, Peter. *The Well-Fed Writer: Financial Self-Sufficiency as a Freelance Writer in Six Months or Less.* Atlanta: Fanove Publishing, 2000.

Bowerman, Peter. *The Well-Fed Writer: Back For Seconds (A Second Helping of "How-To" for Any Writer Dreaming of Great Bucks and Exceptional Quality of Life).* Atlanta: Fanove Publishing, 2005.

Bowerman, Peter. *The Well-Fed Self-Publisher: How to Turn One Book into a Full-Time Living.* Atlanta: Fanove Publishing, 2007.

FOR THE SELF-PUBLISHER

BookMasters, Inc.
www.bookmasters.com
As a printer and distributor, their services include galleys, full printing, fulfillment, storage, and more. As a self-publisher, you may find their services especially helpful for initial documentation, developmental editing, and text and cover design. Give them a call at 800-537-6727, and ask for a self-publishing representative.

Writing World
www.writing-world.com
Great resource with numerous articles about self-publishing
and promoting your book.

Press Release Writing (PRW)
www.press-release-writing.com
Press release writing tips, samples, and expert feedback.

ASSOCIATIONS AND DIRECTORIES

Publisher's Marketing Association (PMA)
www.pma-online.org
A great resource for finding a professional publishing consultant. Note that this association has another business
name. It is the Independent Book Publishers Association.

The Marketing Resource Center (Concept Marketing Group, Inc.)
www.marketingsource.com/associations
Full directory with daily updates, meeting and convention
information, and a powerful search interface.

The Internet Public Library (IPL)
www.ipl.org/div/aon/
A public service organization that provides library services
to Internet users.

Oxbridge Communications, Inc.
www.oxbridge.com
Publishes many directories for media and publishers,
including the *Oxbridge Directory of Newsletters*.

MediaFinder
www.mediafinder.com
Website boasts that they are "the largest database of U.S.
and Canadian periodicals.

Gale Cengage Learning
http://gale.cengage.com/
Visit this site, and view *Gale's Directory*. These electronic resources will allow you to expand and complete your collection of databases.

BOOK CLUBS

Writer's Digest Book Club
www.writersdigestbookclub.com
Forums and resources for writing books.

Literary Market Place
Information Today, Inc.
www.literarymarketplace.com
A great resource book that is updated annually (includes listing of book clubs). Check out this website for an extensive directory of the American book publishing industry.

Book-of-the-Month
www.bomc.com
A vast selection of books.

Quality Paperback Book Club
www.qpb.com
A vast selection of paperbacks.

Doubleday Book Club
www.doubledaybookclub.com
Discounts on publishers' edition book prices.

BOOK REVIEWS IN MAGAZINES

Library Journal
www.libraryjournal.com
With online and printed versions, this industry journal has everything including book news, copyright information, and a membership newsletter.

Booklist
www.ala.org/booklist
American Library Association's (ALA) magazine of book reviews.

Publishers Weekly
www.publishersweekly.com
Simply a must-have for industry insiders.

ForeWord
www.forewordmagazine.com
This magazine focuses on reviewing independently published books.

Kirkus Reviews
www.kirkusreviews.com
Specializes in reviews of fiction, mystery, science fiction, translation, nonfiction, children, and youth books.

BOOKSTORE DATABASES

Biblio Distribution, Inc.
www.bibliodistribution.com
Provides sales and fulfillment services for small presses.

Ingram Book Group
www.ingrambook.com
A huge wholesaler for bookstores.

Baker & Taylor, Inc.
www.btol.com
A wholesaler for libraries, this company boasts that they are the "world's largest book and entertainment distributor."

MAJOR PUBLISHERS

Get a current copy of *Writer's Market* in book format, or research from their online source at **www.writersmarket.com** for specific information on how to approach publishing houses and to learn what kinds of titles they publish.

If you think you've reached that plateau of success where you need to call in the "big guns" to sell your million copies, or if you're just tired of handling all the details, here is a list of some major publishers. Each owns several divisions, which serve different markets.

HarperCollins
www.harpercollins.com
World-famous publishing house.

Holtzbrinck Publishers
www.holtzbrinck.com
Family-owned publisher with headquarters in Germany.

Penguin Group, Inc.
www.penguingroup.com
International publishing house.

Random House, Inc.
www.randomhouse.com
Publisher of fiction, nonfiction, and children's books.

CREATE A WEBSITE

Go Daddy
www.godaddy.com
A great domain-purchasing website. Also offers hosting services and a do-it-yourself application.

Millionaire Blueprints Teen *neither endorses nor recommends any of the companies listed as resources. Resources are intended as a starting point for your research.*

MONEY FOR COLLEGE

GET AN "A" IN FINANCIAL AID

United States college-bound students know that scoring well on tests administered by the College Board is the first step to higher education. For many—perhaps 60 percent to 70 percent of students—obtaining money is next. Head-quartered in New York and consisting of many regional and state offices, the College Board remains a leader in higher education. For information and resources, visit their web-site at **www.collegeboard.com/html/communications000. html#prof**.

Founded in 1900, the not-for-profit College Board's mission is to connect students to college success and opportunity. This membership association is composed of more than 5,200 schools, colleges, universities, and other educational organizations. Annually, it serves seven million students and their parents, 23,000 high schools, and 3,500 colleges through major programs. Its services include college admissions, guidance, assessment, enrollment, teaching, learning, and financial aid.

Among its best-known programs are the Scholastic Aptitude Test (SAT), the Preliminary SAT/National Merit Scholarship Qualifying Test (PSAT/NMSQT), and the Advanced Placement Program (AP). Primers and overviews for each test may be found at the College Board's website.

SAT: **www.collegeboard.com/student/testing/sat/about.html**
PSAT/NMSQT: **www.collegeboard.com/student/testing/ psat/about.html**
AP: **www.collegeboard.com/student/testing/ap/about.html**

HELP IS AT HAND

Cindy Bailey is a College Board executive director specializing in financial aid—usually defined to include student loans. "Help is readily accessible if a student knows where to look," Bailey says. Many high schools even host informational financial aid nights for seniors.

Let's define semantics first: scholarships are considered gift aid and do not need to be paid back. Grants are government-given to low-income students. Self-help aid includes loans.

Want help? "First," Bailey says, "consult your chosen institution's financial aid office, which may funnel up to 90 percent of available funds. Most institutions have a very standard federal program, and schools have their own sources," she says. "Students apply to college and for aid concurrently. Get the information you need from the college, fill out the forms, and wait to be reviewed," she says.

Perhaps the applicant is a violin virtuoso or a star athlete. "Various departments might want that; they control grants that don't go through the financial aid office," Bailey says.

Second, consult your state, since it affords grants and scholarships. Sometimes there are strings attached. For example, you must stay in-state. Do Internet research, beginning with state government. "Adult students may require more resourcefulness to locate these opportunities," Bailey says.

Next, determine outside scholarship viability. "If Dad is in a union, it may offer funding. A financial aid award most frequently entails a loan," Bailey says. "Shop around. The school will have a list of preferred lenders." Even the College Board is a lender. Kids seem to gravitate toward nonprofits. Bailey cites the popular federal U.S. Department of Education Stafford Loan. Get started on your research of federal education loans at **www.ed.gov/finaid/landing.jhtml?src=ln**.

Bailey says that federal government incentives encourage competitive terms from one bank to another.

IT'S OKAY TO ASK FOR AID

Good parent loans exist, too. This is attractive if Mom and Dad don't want to liquidate investments. Rates, terms, and conditions are pretty much the same from one lender to another. Do an Internet search for "federal parent loans," and find programs based on your parents' good credit scores.

Less obvious sources of help may be found in cooperative education programs. This is very typical of engineering and technical schools. "Work a semester; go to school a semester. It's an incredibly good job experience, even if it takes longer," Bailey says. Many leads may be found by starting your own research from the National Commission for Cooperative Education at **www.co-op.edu**.

Consider "Uncle Sam." Take, for example, the military. "You can't beat the Montgomery GI Bill (MGIB) for going back to school," Bailey says. For more information on the MGIB, go to **www.gibill.va.gov/GI_Bill_Info/benefits.htm**.

In addition, Reserve Officer Training Corps (ROTC) programs are lucrative, as former U.S. Secretary of State Colin Powell, actor James Earl Jones, and Wal-Mart founder Sam Walton all know. To learn more on your own about ROTC, go to **https://secure.military.com/Recruiting/requestinfo/rotc/page1.do?ESRC=ggl_rec_rotc.kw&partner=7**.

Expect tuition increases every year, although right now public institutions are hiking costs more than private schools, due, in part, to state budget cuts. What's the cutoff level from "has enough" to "needs more" for college? That's like comparing apples to oranges, Bailey says. Families earning $150,000 annually may apply for aid with two kids in school at $40,000 a year. A family earning $50,000 a year with a student applying to a community college devoid of financial aid, and with $800 tuition, may need aid, too. Everyone's different.

In the 1970s and 1980s, a certain stigma surrounded the practice of applying for aid, which meant a trip to the welfare office. "Times have changed," Bailey says. "No one can really afford to pay out-of-pocket unless they have bottomless bank accounts, or unless their kids attend a very inexpensive school. If they're lucky, the child receives a full merit-based scholarship irrespective of need."

When it comes to finding funds, the same diligence that propels a goal-oriented student into college in the first place may prove invaluable in uncovering financial aid. Where there's a will, there's a way.

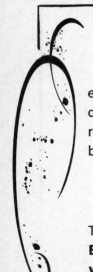

HOW TO WRITE A BLOG

Blogs are a popular marketing tool for businesses and entrepreneurs. Since blogs are updated frequently (often daily or weekly), they provide a unique tactic for gaining repeat visitors and for building a community. Starting a blog is surprisingly simple.

CHOOSE YOUR PLATFORM

A blog platform is the service you use to host your blog. The most popular ones include **www.Wordpress.com**, **www. Blogger.com**, **www.LiveJournal.com**, **www.MySpace.com**, **www.Xanga.com**, and **http://360.yahoo.com**. Research each platform, and choose the one that best fits your blogging needs. The most popular platforms for businesses are WordPress and Blogger.

CHOOSE A THEME

Once you choose your blog platform, make sure you know the purpose of your blog. Will you be posting tips for people in a similar business? Are you interested in sharing opinions about politics or religion? Do you want to give people a glimpse of what you do every day? It might help to look at other blogs for examples of topics you can choose. Just remember that anything you post on the Internet might stay online forever. Even if you delete your post, it will be available for people to view long after your blog is gone if it is captured by a web archive service.

CHOOSE A NAME FOR YOUR BLOG

This is a big decision! Make sure your title is easy to type and easy to remember.

CHOOSE A TEMPLATE

Most platforms offer a variety of templates that you can use as a background for your blog. Don't leave your blog looking plain! Choose a style that reflects your business and that is visually appealing.

CREATE A PROFILE

All blogs include a page where you can share information about yourself. These are usually called profile pages or "About Us" sections. These pages never change. Your profile page should include your name and contact information, information about your business and your website.

POST OFTEN!

Blogs become popular when the user posts frequently. You might want to consider posting daily, if you can. Some blog owners employ multiple writers to ensure that their blog has daily updates.

MARKET YOUR BLOG

After you've made a few posts on your blog, advertise it! Send links to all your friends and customers. Surf the Internet for blogs and forums on similar themes, and post on those sites, leaving links to your blog for responses. If you find a popular blog on a comparable topic, offer to host a link to the blog on your website—if the user will also host a link to your blog.

MONITOR YOUR COMMENTS

Blogs include a space after each post for comments. To keep your blog active, you will want to respond to comments left on your blog with comments of your own.

Remember the "golden rule" of the blogging world: If you want people to leave comments on your blog, leave comments on their blogs first.

INCREASE TRAFFIC TO YOUR BLOG

Blog traffic takes time to build. Don't get discouraged if you see only a few comments at first. One popular method for increasing traffic to your blog is by visiting social websites such as Digg.com. If you post an interesting news story or comment, you can submit a link to Digg. You can also install a "Digg this" button under newsworthy posts on your blog so readers can submit your post if they wish.

An additional way to drive traffic to your blog is by using "tags." These are keywords related to your subject that are used by search engines. Finally, you can increase traffic by claiming your blog on Technorati (**http://technorati.com**). Technorati is a blog search engine.

PING WHEN YOU POST

Every time you add a post to your blog, you should "ping" the post on search engines. This is a protocol that sends a message to another computer and waits for acknowledgment. You can use an automatic service such as **http://pingoat.com** or **http://pingomatic.com**.

UTILIZE RSS FEEDS

Install an RSS (Really Simple Syndication) button on your blog so readers can subscribe and be notified whenever you add a new post. You can visit the About.com section on RSS for more information.

A FEW TIPS BEFORE YOU START

Always monitor your comments! Many people will spam blogs to leave information about their businesses or just to be obnoxious.

Be careful what you post! Once you become involved in the world of blogging, you will find it very tempting to post information about yourself that is too personal. Always ask yourself if your post is appropriate for your blogging goals.

Consider whether you want to include advertising in your blog. Some people use programs such as Google Adsense, which posts ads on your blog related to your posts and pays you every time someone clicks on the ad.

If you find that you love blogging, you might want to look into paid blogging opportunities. Many companies offer jobs for professional bloggers.

CHAPTER 4

Ben
CATHERS

He yearned for a CEO's desk, and he had nothing to lose.

BUSINESS NAME(S):
Search Rate Technologies, LLC
A2Connect, LLC

BUSINESS TYPE(S):
Internet Search Engine Technology
Wireless Media Marketing

LOCATION:
Boston, MA

When he was twelve years old, Ben Cathers knew he wanted to be a businessman. He realized that no one was going to hire him for the office job he longed for, so he thought he'd better create his own opportunities. His parents had to sign contracts for him because of his age, but their support was a perfect launching pad to some "phat" profits.

The young business owner built his online game portal network, called PhatStart.com, into a marketing cash cow. He became such a powerhouse at his young age that Silicon Alley Reporter magazine named his company one of the "top twelve" to look out for.

After selling his first company, and getting his message over the radio waves as cofounder and CEO of the Teen American Media Group, he left for college and started all over again. He was also the executive producer and cofounder of Klick-TV, and the cofounder of Search Rate Technologies (**www.searchratetechnologies.com**). No matter what he does, it seems that Ben Cathers was truly born to be a CEO. Today, Ben is based in Boston and keeps his entrepreneurial muscles in shape by working with a wide variety of young technology start-up companies.

The joy he got as a twelve-year-old when he purchased his Forbes magazine at the newsstand is eclipsed only by the excitement he recently dished to Millionaire Blueprints Teen over obtaining Smashing Pumpkins concert tickets . . . three nights in a row. It's good to have connections! Right, Ben?

GETTING STARTED IN BUSINESS

How did your business life begin?

I started playing with web text when I was twelve years old. Soon after, I started the PhatStart.com network that included PhatGames.com for news and entertainment, as well as PhatGames.net. I earned a reputation as a young businessman before selling this online network.

What were some of the challenges that led to your success?

That was when you paid hourly on AOL, and you had to pay to play games online. I would search the web, but there wasn't a central directory. I would first find directories and then portals to free games online.

So, your website addressed these inadequacies?

Yes, and it grew really quickly because people wanted to play games online for free. When the bandwidth got too expensive, I needed a sponsor.

How did you get sponsors?

An advertising agency helped me sell ads on the website. There were so many advertisers that we didn't have enough space. I decided to partner with similar websites, so we started selling advertising for those sites, as well.

It sounds like the size of your business increased rapidly.

We incorporated the business when I was thirteen years old and were considered one of the top twelve companies to look for by the *Silicon Alley Reporter*.

So, how many ads did you sell on your site?

We had 300 million advertisements a month. The advertisements were from a variety of different advertisers. We were one of the top five teen advertising networks at the time. I had seven employees with two offices. After four years, I sold to the ad company we had been working with.

Did you retire?

I wanted to save the last two years of my teens, but I was only out of the business for two months before I started the radio show *Teen America*. I was seventeen, on the air for a year and a half, and even got picked up by a syndicator called PCBroadcast.com (now called New Broadcast, Inc.). We received clearance on various ABC stations. We were webcast in fifty countries, and on Long Island. We were going coast to coast, but we needed to upgrade our studio and hire a new host. Then, one of our investors died, the station went bankrupt, and it didn't happen. We didn't have the money, ourselves, when our investor died.

The show ended, and then what did you do?

I was a business student at Boston University on an academic scholarship, focusing on entrepreneurship. They offer about eight or nine entrepreneurship classes. The relationships I made were the best. There were young entrepreneurs and professors there who advise me to this day. The teachers weren't scholars, but they all had built and sold companies.

Shortly after arriving at school, I did some consulting with start-up businesses. I also created a search engine software company with another classmate, Gavin Durni. It is called Search Rate Technologies, LLC. It was a human-rated search engine where people could rate things—and change the way things were rated. At that time, we received a $100,000 check from angel investors to pay for the programming. We raised more financing, but we couldn't compete against Google. So, it became a business search engine. I was offered a buyout in the new funding search, so I accepted.

What do you do these days?

I am on the team of a wireless marketing company, A2Connect (**www.A2Connect.com**). We provide wireless marketing for affinity groups.

What is an affinity group?

They are self-supporting groups of people that are working toward a common goal.

How do you network?

I use LinkedIn to network online (**www.linkedin.com**). I also go to local events like the Massachusetts Institute of Technology's (MIT) Enterprise Forum (**http://enterpriseforum.mit.edu**), and ONEin3 Boston (**www.onein3boston.org**), which is an excellent local networking group that has been helpful. Boston University's Corporate Education Center (**www.butrain.com**) has a lot of events that are open to anybody.

The best thing to do when you meet someone new is to ask questions about the person's business and let them talk. Everyone loves to talk about their company. Once you've established a connection with the person, exchange business cards. Tell them how you think your companies could benefit each other.

What is a networking highlight you can share?

I was at this party at the Playboy Mansion and met the famous poker player Jamie Gold. He is the 2006 World Series of Poker champion. I told him that I was a huge fan, that I was part of a wireless company, and that we wanted to have a wireless product around his name. You always have to be working the business; you have to approach any option. We have gotten better support from investors since we linked up with Jamie Gold.

What inspired you, at age nineteen, to write your book Conversations with Teen Entrepreneurs?

I wrote my book because I wanted to legitimize the fact that teen entrepreneurs are for real. I wanted to show what people can do.

How did you publish your book?

I used iUniverse.com, and they made the self-publishing experience flawlessly simple for me. They offer various publishing packages, ranging from a $399 fee up to $1,399. They provide editorial and marketing services, and they print on demand. iUniverse pays its authors a royalty of 20 percent on print sales and 50 percent on e-book sales. If you're an established author, you have a chance at negotiating your percentage.

What was your biggest failure?

When you fail, you hit rock bottom. It's not fun. But it's great because you've felt the pain, and you're never going to let it happen again. You will never make that same mistake because you remember how much it hurt. I failed once by hiring the wrong assistant. I failed in raising capital. But I saw the factors that led to the failure, and I made sure to avoid them later.

What is your schedule like these days?

In addition to my daily work at A2Connect, I speak at industry events on entrepreneurship in the Boston community. I contribute to panels, and I help mentor students. I still design websites. I use Jumpline.com for webhosting.

THE MARKETING

What was your first experience with marketing?

We could purchase a large number of ads that would be seen by anyone who visited the website. I was young and inexperienced and just saw the bargain basement cost.

Did that work out for you?

I committed a sin that many small businesses commit. I strayed from my target audience. It ended up being a $2,500 mistake. You must determine to whom you are marketing and to whom your advertisements are directed.

How does someone determine what part of their budget should go toward advertising?

Determine how much of a necessity the product is and how loyal your customers are. Look at what competitors are doing, and make a decision based on those results. If you are a new business, you will need to put a significant portion into getting your name out.

Word of mouth, trade shows and conferences, networking groups, press articles, print advertising, web advertising, and e-mail are other methods that have brought success to some.

What about online marketing?

One of the best methods of finding information on the Internet is through search engines.

THE INTERNET

Speaking of search engines, what is a "web presence"?

It is a very important part of your business. The first thing to do is to get a domain name, which is your business name, to be used as the component of your website's uniform resource locator (URL). It can cost as little as six dollars and ninety-nine cents. You can use GoDaddy.com or Web.com.

What tips can you give those who are setting up websites?

First of all, make full use of the <meta> description and keywords. The <meta> element provides information about your website, such as keywords and descriptions for search engines. Ask your web designer if you don't understand. Make sure your description is around twenty words, and that the keywords of your site are around twenty to thirty words. You want to start buying keywords on search engines. Also, look around at other sites in the market, and look at the advertising rates. Try to get your website on as many other sites as possible to generate traffic.

What other ways do you use the Internet for business processes besides marketing?

There are many free and low-cost solutions out there. For example, instant messaging (IM) has mostly been used by people who want to stay in touch with one another. If used correctly, it is an invaluable tool for business. There must be ground rules, of course. This is true of e-mail as well.

What should someone have on their website?

Content is one of the most important items a website can have. By helping to educate the user about the services a business provides, or about information pertaining to the industry, you are helping the visitor gain knowledge. This adds extra value to the website and gives you an advantage over competitors. Also, make sure it is updated regularly. Visitors want content that is current. It is a good idea to learn programming language called "hypertext markup language" (HTML). To learn about it, visit my favorite site, HTMLGoodies.com.

Do most people need an in-house web team, or do freelancers work just as well?

Businesses that rely heavily on their websites should have an in-house web team. This could mean anywhere from 1 to 100 people whose primary job is to maintain the website. This is important if the site requires daily updates and additions. If a business decides to outsource, this can cost anywhere from $100 to $100,000, and more. Sometimes it works to have a combination of both when you have it designed by a firm, and you are also trained to maintain the site.

What is a webhost, and how does someone choose one?

The webhost is where the website of a business is located. Depending on the needs of your business, webspace with a webhost can be from one dollar and ninety-nine cents per month to almost $100 a month. The best places to look are HostingCatalog.com (formerly ISPCheck.com) and HostSearch.com.

THE SALES

How does someone turn a web visitor into a client?

Treat the visitor as a potential customer. For instance, when visitors come into a store to take a look around, they are there because they are interested in the products/services offered. Don't undermine their intelligence by inundating them with pop-up ads. You can add value to your website by having a product or service that people can purchase from you online.

How do you approach new corporate clients?

Research the company, the industry, and the needs. Research the competitors. The potential client will be impressed. In addition, you will be able to offer solutions relevant to the client. You might want to role-play with a colleague to prepare.

THE LEGAL

Who takes care of your finances?

My personal accountant, Doug Murstein (**www.dougjmurstein cpa.com**), and my financial adviser assist with my investments. This includes stocks, mutual funds, savings bonds, and more. Contact Jessica Piemonte, who is a financial adviser specializing in global wealth management. (**NOTE:** Her contact information is in the resources section.)

What about legal advice?

I took some contracts classes in college, so I learned how to write my own contracts. However, I use different local lawyers for various projects that I am involved in.

THE MONEY

How do you approach investors?

In the case of an original investor, I say throw all your pride away. Give them a reason why you're going to do what you're going to do. Show them what you've learned from mistakes and why you need more money. When you're in the start-up stage of your company and are approaching investors, not everything will happen the way you want it to. Not everything will fall into place as planned. You need to show that you realize this, that you made mistakes and that you have researched all possible alternatives to fix the mistakes. Tell potential investors that it will cost them this much money, and that it will bring back this much. They want their company to increase in value.

As for new investors, show them the solutions. Show them that you've thought about everything that could happen. Use customer testimonials, show quotes, and show a demonstrated need for your product. Show that the market requires a solution like the one you have. If you can show a product that is highly marketable, they will listen to you.

You need to provide new investors with a way that can get them a 100-percent to 300-percent return in profit. It's very risky to put money into a start-up company. They can buy a certificate of deposit (CD) and get 5 percent, which involves little risk. Investors usually agree if the risk is only 10 percent to 15 percent—but with an 80 percent to 90 percent risk, they will only agree to invest in your company if they can make huge percentages in profit. Show why your product will be such a hot property that Google will want to buy it as well.

If you are going to sell the company, you will ultimately have to show how they will get their money back. People have to put themselves in the investor's seat. You're asking them to put money into a market they don't understand, and they won't have it back for several months. And, they want to know if you put your money in, too. This is a big selling point with investors. Otherwise, there's no risk for you.

What mistake do you see some people make with investors?

Figuring out the equipment and technology issues is necessary. When investors request a business plan, you need to make sure it is in a compatible format. Sending your files in a portable document format (PDF) keeps your original document intact and is the cure-all for any questionable tampering issues for any type of written document. Saving and sending your documents in a PDF solves any questions regarding compatibility, because it makes your documents viewable from any application on any computer system. Also, you should always follow up with any requests for information after the initial meeting.

Who were the first people you approached?

I approached the firm, Wall Street Venture Capital. They realized I was young, and they treated me with care. They said, "No." But they explained why. This was extremely important, because it helped me improve. I went back, and they passed again. So, I kept shopping it around.

Where does your money come from now?

I receive income from investments and consultant fees, and I am part of four companies. I draw money from two of them.

This Smashing Pumpkins lovin', Playboy Mansion visiting, money-making entrepreneur has certainly made a big impression in the business world. He's progressed from being a kid who buys his favorite business periodicals, to appearing repeatedly in the hottest business publications. The possibilities are unlimited for this author, entrepreneur, and business owner.

THE PLAN TO FOLLOW

STEP 1

Approach investors to fund your start-up company or to give added capital to your established business. Do your market research, and reduce the percentage of risk for potential investors.

NOTE: Be confident in your product and in your strategies. Show them what your company is all about with visuals and well-researched market data. Cathers says, "Throw all your pride away. Give them a reason why you're going to do what you're going to do." They may say, "No." If they do, learn why, and fix the problem before you ask again.

STEP 2

Network at industry events, and meet someone new.

NOTE: Cathers advises that the best thing to do when you meet someone new is to ask questions about the person's business, and let them talk. He says, "Everyone loves to talk about their company. Once you've established a connection with the person, exchange business cards. Tell them how you think your companies could benefit each other."

STEP 3

Determine to whom you are marketing and to whom your advertisements are directed.

STEP 4

Decide what part of your budget will go to advertising. Establish how much of a necessity the product is and how loyal your customers are. Look at what competitors are doing, and make a decision based on those results.

NOTE: Cathers stresses that, if you are a new business, you will need to put a significant portion of your budget into getting your name out to the public. Word of mouth, trade shows and conferences, networking groups, press articles, print advertising, web advertising, and e-mail are all good options.

THE HIGHLIGHTS

- You always have to be working the business; you have to approach any option.
- Recognize factors that lead to failure, learn from mistakes, and avoid those factors in the future.
- Never stray from your intended target audience—it could be a costly mistake.
- Establish a web presence with a unique domain name. Use keywords wisely to maximize search engine optimization.
- Create exceptional and current web content—both are essential to conducting business on the Internet.

THE RESOURCES

Ben Cathers
www.bencathers.com/about.html
The official biographical website for this young entrepreneur.

SearchRate Technologies, LLC
www.searchratetechnologies.com
Ben Cathers is the chief operating officer. The company is changing the way search engine technology works by "developing a new search engine that hopes to bring searching and indexing back to the original roots of the Internet."

A2Connect, LLC
www.A2Connect.com
Ben Cathers is the project manager for this wireless marketing company, specializing in multimedia wireless communication for affinity groups. (To learn more, click on the "Affinity Programs" tab from the homepage.)

Cathers, Ben. *Conversations with Teen Entrepreneurs: Success Secrets of the Younger Generation*. Lincoln, NE: iUniverse, Inc., 2003.

SELF-PUBLISHING

iUniverse, Inc.
www.iuniverse.com
Print-on-demand, self-publishing company. Offers various publishing packages, editorial and marketing services, and has a "strategic alliance with Barnes & Noble."

WEBHOSTING

Jumpline.com
www.jumpline.com
Provides various webhosting plans, using virtual dedicated server (VDS) technology for reliability and security.

iNET Interactive
Hosting Catalog
www.hostingcatalog.com
Offers advanced webhosting and shared webhosting products and services, in addition to connectivity information, domain registration, and merchant accounts.

Clicksee Network Company, Ltd.
HostSearch
www.hostsearch.com
It's all about webhosting here, including promotions for members, articles, forums, a quote wizard, tutorials, and more.

MISCELLANEOUS RESOURCES

GoDaddy.com, Inc.
www.godaddy.com
Offers low-cost services for domains, webhosting and servers, website construction, e-mail, e-commerce, and much more.

Web.com, Inc.
www.web.com
Offers website solutions for a variety of integrated online tools and services, including website design and web publishing, webhosting, business e-mail, domain name registration, web marketing, and e-commerce—all specifically designed for small business owners with novice design and technical skills.

LinkedIn Corporation
www.linkedin.com
Professional online network full of inside connections, industry experts, and business advice.

Jupitermedia Corporation
HTMLGoodies.com
www.htmlgoodies.com
A favorite of Cathers, this site will assist you in learning the language of programmers and hypertext markup language (HTML). This site is helpful to beginners and experienced website developers by providing tips, guides, references, and more.

INDUSTRY EVENTS AND NETWORKING GROUPS

Massachusetts Institute of Technology (MIT)
Enterprise Forum, Inc.
http://enterpriseforum.mit.edu
Anyone is welcome to participate in this technology network that produces a series of educational programs about entrepreneurship among twenty-four chapters worldwide.

ONEin3 Boston
www.onein3boston.org
Program is for young people between the ages of twenty and thirty-four, and connects them "with resources related to home buying, business development, professional networking, and civic engagement."

Boston University Corporate Education Center
www.butrain.com
Offers training and certification programs, various events, and online seminars. Click on the "Technology Programs" link to learn more.

VENTURE CAPITAL FIRM

Wall Street Venture Capital
www.wallstreetventurecapital.net
Firm dedicated to helping entrepreneurs specializing in networking, broadcasting, computer software, electronic equipment and components, entertainment, and more.

FINANCIAL HELP

Doug Murstein, Certified Public Accountant (CPA)
www.dougjmursteincpa.com
Cathers's personal accountant who specializes in individual and corporate tax return preparation, accounting and bookkeeping services, business start-up advice, and small business consulting.

Merrill Lynch, Pierce, Fenner & Smith, Inc.
Jessica Piemonte
Global Wealth Management
www.fa.ml.com/JESSICA_PIEMONTE
Cathers' financial adviser who assists with his investments, including stocks, mutual funds, savings bonds, and more.

Millionaire Blueprints Teen *neither endorses nor recommends any of the companies listed as resources. Resources are intended as a starting point for your research.*

BUSINESS STRUCTURES PRIMER

BY STEPHANIE STEPHENS

When starting a business, one of the most important decisions you make is what type of legal structure you select for your company. The type of legal structure determines what you pay in taxes, what paperwork you are required to complete, and what impact you may face regarding personal liability.

FOUR TYPES OF BUSINESS STRUCTURES
SOLE PROPRIETORSHIP

A sole proprietorship is an unincorporated business that legally has no separate existence from its owner. This is the simplest form of a business organization. All expenses and income of the business are included on your own tax return.

A sole proprietorship can operate out of a personal bank account, using the person's name as the business. To operate under a name other than your own, you must first go to your local courthouse and fill out the paperwork for an Assumed Name Certificate, also known as a Doing Business As (DBA) Certificate. Take this DBA Certificate with you when you go to the bank. You must place a copy of it on file with your bank in order to open an account. Then, you can order company checks with your DBA business name imprinted on them.

Advantages of a Sole Proprietorship

Sole proprietors remain in complete control—without much exposure to liability.

Tax advantages include an avoidance of a double tax, and business losses can be deducted based on the extent of your total income from all sources.

If necessary, the business is easy to dissolve.

Disadvantages of a Sole Proprietorship

The sole proprietor is personally liable for all the debts of the business. Both personal and business assets are at risk.

The sole proprietor can transfer the business only by the sale of business assets, making it difficult to have someone buy into the business.

There are tax penalties for switching a sole proprietorship to a corporation or a limited liability company (LLC).

GENERAL PARTNERSHIP

A general partnership is a corporation formed by two or more people, with all owners held liable for legal actions and debts the company may face. A partnership agreement states the manner in which profits and losses are to be shared.

Advantages of a General Partnership

Partnerships can be relatively cheap and are easy to form and maintain.

The partnership, itself, is not taxed. The partners are taxed as individuals.

The profits from the business are directed to the partners' personal tax returns.

Disadvantages of a General Partnership

A general partner has unlimited personal liability for the business.

Obtaining long-term financing is often difficult for smaller partnerships.

The partnership can end due to a dissemination or the death of a partner.

CORPORATION

A corporation is a legal entity created by law that is composed of individuals united under a common name. Empowered with legal rights, the members create an organization that hires employees, obtains loans, contracts obligations, grants property, and exercises a variety of political rights.

Advantages of a Corporation

Corporations have an unlimited life. If the owner decides to leave, the company will still exist and do business.

Shareholders have limited liability for the corporation's debts.

Ownership of the corporation can be sold through sale of stock.

Disadvantages of a Corporation

The process of incorporation requires a lot of time and money. It can be very complex.

Since corporations are monitored by federal and state agencies, you must comply with all legal formalities.

Incorporating results in higher overall taxes.

LIMITED LIABILITY COMPANY (LLC)

An LLC combines the most attractive features of partnerships and corporations but isn't classified as one or the other. The number of members is unlimited and may include individuals, corporations, or other LLCs. Members enjoy the limited liability offered by a corporate form of ownership and the tax advantages of a partnership.

Advantages of an LLC

Owners of an LLC have the liability protection of a corporation. Members cannot be held personally liable for debts.

Owners have limited personal liability for business debts, even if they participate in management.

LLCs avoid the double taxation of paying corporate and individual taxes.

Disadvantages of an LLC

LLCs are more expensive to create than a partnership or a sole proprietorship.

LLCs dissolve if a member dies or goes bankrupt.

Special care is required in establishing the LLC to make sure the preferred tax status is attained.

SETTING UP YOUR BUSINESS STRUCTURE

You've chosen a business structure. Now what? How do you make it official? What documents have to be filled out and filed, and with what agency? Let's take a look at what an Internet survey revealed.

SETTING UP A SOLE PROPRIETORSHIP

STEP 1

Check your state's guidelines to find out if you need a business or professional license. (See the "Check State Guidelines and Procedures" section in this chapter.)

STEP 2

To operate under a name other than your own, you need to notify the county of the state where the business is located. You'll need to fill out a form (usually one page) and pay a fee. The form has different names in different states (for example, Assumed Name Certificate, Doing Business As (DBA), or Fictitious Business Name Statement). Whichever one your county uses, they all ask for the same general information. Contact the local county clerk's office, or look for it online to find forms, filing fees, and where to file. Make sure to check to see if your state requires any scheduled updates in the future.

STEP 3

Request certified copies of the form if the county clerk keeps the original. You'll need one for the bank and one for your records.

SETTING UP A GENERAL PARTNERSHIP

STEP 1

Draw up, and sign a partnership agreement. You can create your own, or you can consult an attorney to help you with this. Make sure to outline how all potential business scenarios will be handled. In addition, you may have to register a Partnership Certificate or an Assumed Name Certificate with the county. (**NOTE:** An Assumed Name Certificate is one possible name for your state's required form in order to operate your business under a name other than your own.)

STEP 2

Obtain a business or professional license. (See also the "Check State Guidelines and Procedures" section in this chapter.)

SETTING UP A CORPORATION, A LIMITED LIABILITY COMPANY (LLC), A SMALL BUSINESS (S-CORPORATION), AND A NON-PROFIT

STEP 1

Every state sets its own rules and regulations for the process of incorporating. They all require filling out and filing a Certificate of Incorporation, or Articles of Incorporation, and paying one or more fees. Corporate existence begins when the paperwork is filed, along with the required fees.

STEP 2

To form a partnership, an LLC, or a corporation, it is wise to consult with an attorney to ensure that all details are in order. To incorporate your business, you or your attorney must contact the relevant Secretary of State's office to get the forms and paperwork you will need to fill out. Then, file those with the state.

It is very important for business owners to seek expert advice from professionals when considering the pros and cons of business structures—whether it be an attorney, an accountant, a financial adviser, a banker, or any other legal adviser. Keep in mind that you can always change your business structure if your business grows or if your need to limit your personal liability increases.

If you want to try to do this yourself, *Millionaire Blueprints Teen* has found some companies that say they will help you incorporate over the Internet or by telephone. They can help you with as few, or as many, of the steps as you'd like. Here are some of those companies:

American Incorporators Ltd.
www.ailcorp.com
800-421-2661
This company provides a comprehensive range of formation and corporate compliance services for all fifty states.

Corporate Creations
www.corpcreations.com
800-672-9110
This company has statutory registered offices nationwide and offshore. They offer registered agents and entity filing services.

BizFilings
www.bizfilings.com
800-981-7183
This company's services are for corporations, LLCs, small businesses, and non-profits. They also offer a rush service filing option in less than one day.

The Company Corporation
www.corporate.com
800-818-0204
This company offers nationwide registered agent services. Its website provides an interactive start-up wizard to help you understand your needs, as well as a quarterly online newsletter.

Companies Incorporated
www.companiesinc.com
800-830-1055
This company offers complete filing support and customer service nationwide.

American Corporate Register, Inc.
www.incnevada.com
800-944-1120
This company specializes in Nevada incorporation. According to its website, many people choose to incorporate in Nevada because of the state's tax breaks and privacy.

Corporation Makers, Inc.
www.corpmakers.com
800-267-7657
This company specializes in the Nevada and California incorporation process.

Millionaire Blueprints Teen *neither endorses nor recommends any of the companies listed as resources. Resources are intended as a starting point for your research.*

HOW TO INCORPORATE

STEP 1
Decide Who Will Do the Paperwork

You have three options: you can do it yourself, hire a company that specializes in filing incorporation papers, or hire an attorney. Research the process and your options to become informed about what needs to be done and the decisions you'll need to make, even if you plan to hire someone. Look for books at your local bookstore, or search any of the online booksellers by typing in the words, "how to incorporate."

Hiring an attorney usually costs more than the other options. When starting a business, you're in "the deep end of the pool," so to speak, and it's good to have a "lifeguard" looking out for you.

Even if you plan to file the paperwork yourself, you can hire an attorney for a couple of hours to make sure you've thought things through. The more complex your business is, or will be, the more you need to get it right from the beginning. Get a referral from a friend, a network group, or an attorney who does other types of work. You can also find an attorney by searching online or in the local *Yellow Pages*. Look for one who's reputable and who specializes in this field.

STEP 2
Choose a Name

Most state guidelines say your business name must look and sound different from existing companies. Also, it cannot mislead the public. When you incorporate, most states require you to add "Corp.," "Inc.," or something similar to the end of your business name. If you need help choosing a name, there are several books and online resources on the topic.

Check out Creative Ways' website at **www.yudkin.com/ generate.htm**. Here you will find Marcia Yudkin's advice. Read her article the Business Name & Tag Line Generator.

You may also want to look into hiring experts to choose a business name for you. Start researching this option at the NameStormers' website at **www.namestormers.com**.

STEP 3
Check Name Availability

Your paperwork will be returned if the name is already in use, so check before you send it in. Also, by doing a thorough search, you can avoid legal issues down the road. Type the name into several online search engines, and then check at the county level for local companies that aren't listed online. Your county clerk's office can steer you in the right direction. They might also do the search for you for a small fee, as will the online incorporation companies. Most importantly, don't purchase anything with your new name on it until your incorporation papers are approved. The state will do a name search too. If you missed it, or if someone submitted the same name just before you, you'll be out some money.

STEP 4
Decide in Which State to Incorporate

Most businesses incorporate in the state where their home office is. However, it's not required. You might want to incorporate in another state because of favorable corporate laws, tax benefits, and income taxes. If you're considering this, consult an attorney who is familiar with foreign corporation rules. Your company is considered "foreign" when you operate in a state other than the one in which you incorporated. If you choose this option, know that the paperwork is more complex, that there are more rules to follow, and that you'll be paying fees in multiple states. But it can be worth the extra effort and money.

STEP 5
Check State Guidelines and Procedures

Every state now has a website that you can find by going to any online search engine and typing in "state of (your state's name)." The Internal Revenue Service also has a page with links to all fifty states. You can find it by going to the Internal Revenue Service's website at **www.irs.gov**, clicking on "Businesses," then on "Starting a Business," and finally on "State Links." Once you get to your state's website, type "starting a business" in the search box. You can also search for "Articles of Incorporation" or "Business Forms." Another option is to call the relevant Secretary of State to help you find this information.

STEP 6
Fill Out Incorporation Forms

In most states, you will need to provide the following information: company name, number of shares (and their values), name and address of a registered agent, name and address of the director, name(s) and address(es) of incorporator(s), and the effective date of the filing. If you plan to issue shares of different classes, you'll need to provide detailed information on each. (**NOTE:** This document becomes a matter of public record.)

Most states require you to have a registered agent in the state where you incorporate. Its purpose is to have someone available to receive legal and tax documents for your

READER/CUSTOMER CARE SURVEY

HEFT

We care about your opinions! Please take a moment to fill out our online Reader Survey at **http://survey.hcibooks.com.**
As a **"THANK YOU"** you will receive a **VALUABLE INSTANT COUPON** towards future book purchases as well as a **SPECIAL GIFT** available only online! Or, you may mail this card back to us and we will send you a copy of our exciting catalog with your valuable coupon inside.

(PLEASE PRINT IN ALL CAPS)

First Name		MI.	Last Name

Address			City

State	Zip	Email:

1. Gender
- ❏ Female
- ❏ Male

2. Age
- ❏ 8 or younger
- ❏ 9-12
- ❏ 13-16
- ❏ 17-20
- ❏ 21-30
- ❏ 31+

3. Did you receive this book as a gift?
- ❏ Yes
- ❏ No

4. How did you find out about the book
- ❏ School
- ❏ Friend
- ❏ Parent

- ❏ Online
- ❏ Store Display
- ❏ Teen Magazine
- ❏ Interview/Review

5. Where do you usually buy books *(please choose one)*
- ❏ Bookstore
- ❏ Online
- ❏ Book Club/Mail Order
- ❏ Price Club (Sam's Club, Costco's, etc.)
- ❏ Retail Store (Target, Wal-Mart, etc.)

6. What magazines do you like to read *(please choose one)*
- ❏ Teen People
- ❏ Seventeen
- ❏ YM
- ❏ Cosmo Girl
- ❏ Rolling Stone
- ❏ Teen Ink
- ❏ Christian Magazines

7. What books do you like to read *(please choose one)*
- ❏ Fiction
- ❏ Self-help
- ❏ Reality Stories/Memoirs
- ❏ Sports
- ❏ Series Books (Chicken Soup, Fearless, etc.)

8. What attracts you most to a book *(please choose one)*
- ❏ Title
- ❏ Cover Design
- ❏ Author
- ❏ Content

TAPE IN MIDDLE; DO NOT STAPLE

BUSINESS REPLY MAIL
FIRST-CLASS MAIL PERMIT NO 45 DEERFIELD BEACH, FL

POSTAGE WILL BE PAID BY ADDRESSEE

HCI Teens
3201 SW 15th Street
Deerfield Beach FL 33442-9875

FOLD HERE

Comments

company on any business day. A registered agent must have a street address (not a post office box). Generally, the registered agent's office must be open during normal business hours. Some states allow you to be your own registered agent. But, according to SCORE (**www.score.org/leg_ registered_agent**), there are three reasons why it's better to use a reliable third party. First, it allows you to be out of the office, including vacations. This is good for small business owners. Second, if you are ever involved in legal issues, you won't be served in front of your clients, vendors, or neighbors. And third, you can move your office without having to file change of address forms with your state.

If you do use a service company, look for one that has offices nationwide, so it can still help you when you grow. Most companies that provide incorporation services will perform this duty for an extra fee. They can do so even if you don't hire them to file the incorporation papers.

You have the option to request a delayed effective date. Some states let you choose an effective date other than the date you are filing (usually, it must be within ninety days). Your corporation is not legally in existence until this date. If you're filing close to the end of the year, this might allow you the following benefits: to avoid being taxed in the current calendar year, to avoid needing to file an annual report for the current calendar year, and to avoid the new year's backlog by having your paperwork processed early.

STEP 7
Send in Forms and Filing Fees

State filing fees range from $1 to $350, so check your state's website. You may also search many of the incorporation companies' websites. Most of them have a handy lookup feature for finding fees. For a table including all state filing fees, visit BizFilings' website at **www.bizfilings.com/ pricing/index.html**. By clicking on the individual states in the table, you can also access some state-specific information. (**NOTE:** You may also be required to pay franchise taxes when you file.)

STEP 8
Wait for Approval

Once all of the necessary paperwork is filed, the approval process generally takes four to six weeks, though some states have expedited processing, which may shorten the time to seven to ten days or less. Once the documents have been checked and deemed complete, the state will send back evidence of your filing—and you're on your way. Some states still require a published notice in a newspaper that your corporation has been formed. So, check your state's guidelines.

STEP 9
Time to Do More Research!

Now that your corporation is set up, you will need to begin adhering to the guidelines set forth by your state regarding shares, meetings, and record keeping. Do an Internet search using those business keywords to get started.

Setting up the business structure is just one of the many first steps required in starting your own company. Other things to consider may include employer requirements, getting an Employer Identification Number (EIN), and tax responsibilities—including sales tax. Learn even more by checking your state's website and the U.S. Small Business Administration's (SBA) website.

MORE RESOURCES

U.S. Small Business Administration (SBA)
www.sba.gov/hotlist/license.html
SBA Answer Desk: 800-827-5722
E-mail: answerdesk@sba.gov
This link allows you to search business licensing information for every state. (**NOTE:** Go back to the homepage
[**www.sba.gov**], and spend some time reviewing the wide
assortment of information available on this website.)

SCORE
www.score.org
As a resource partner with the SBA, this nonprofit association provides entrepreneur education for the formation,
growth, and success of small businesses nationwide.
SCORE offers free and confidential small business advice
for entrepreneurs.

U.S. Department of the Treasury
Internal Revenue Service (IRS)
www.irs.gov
This website is a storehouse of information. Spend time
here, and research thoroughly. The answers to your
many business concerns may be found.

FreeAdvice
www.freeadvice.com
Obtain free legal advice here on business law and more.

The Wall Street Journal
http://online.wsj.com/small-business
Formerly known as the Startup Journal, this link takes you to the *Wall Street Journal* and its online information for small businesses. Offers a blog, feature articles, small business reports, numerous links, various columns, and instructional and informative tool kits.

Entrepreneur.com, Inc.
www.entrepreneur.com
Everything you ever wanted to know about being a successful entrepreneur—and about enjoying your success—may be found on this reputable website.

Millionaire Blueprints Teen *neither endorses nor recommends any of the companies listed as resources. Resources are intended as a starting point for your research.*

HOW TO BUILD YOUR OWN WEBSITE

PROSPECTING FOR GOLD, AND CASHING IN ON MARKETING IN THE INTERNET ERA

You may think the now-famous three letters, *www* just stand for World Wide Web. Allow us to point out that, with its scarcity of regulatory laws and the ability to do just about anything you can dream up, much of this still uncharted territory may sometimes feel more like the wild, wild West. While we entertain you with a few undeniable parallels, just remember that there's definitely "gold in them there hills" and that *Millionaire Blueprints Teen* is here to help you pack the prospecting tools you'll need for an exciting—if not technologically harrowing—journey.

Companies stake claim to large tracts, and then lease them out in little pieces. There are plenty of honest, hard-working pioneers—and also more than a few shady characters hawking the high-tech equivalent of snake oil. Use this article and its accompanying resources to explore some helpful links before you begin. And, while the details and possibilities are fairly endless, we hope the following information will equip you to begin your own exploration of a wild frontier.

MAP YOUR JOURNEY

Where will you begin? Start with the most important element—your audience. Do a complete analysis of what your customers will expect from your website and what will appeal to them. If you're not sure how to figure this out, find companies that market to your typical customers and visit their sites. If everyone is a potential customer, then look at the sites of large companies that market to everyone. What's the best way to start thinking like a customer? Be one. Surf the web, and look for sites that you like—and, just as important, sites you don't.

Check out *PC Magazine*'s picks for the top 100 classic and top 100 undiscovered websites for the year 2007 at **www.pcmag.com/category2/0,4148,7488,00.asp**. Look for sites with a purpose similar to yours. They don't have to be in the same industry—or even the same size. Just pick a few that are attractive to you, and then dissect these sites, element by element. Look at all the buttons, features, and images. Click on each section. What does each do? What color schemes do you like? How simple or complex are the pages? How easily do they load? Make a list of all the features you find that you'd like to have on your site. And, if you're starting small, make two lists: one for now and one to grow into. Be the consumer. Pay attention to what works and what doesn't. Then, envision your ideal site and write it all down.

ASSEMBLE YOUR PROVISIONS

What are you going to need? This step can be tedious, but worthwhile. Get out some paper and a pencil, and map out your website. Use a flowchart, or a series of connected boxes, showing the sequence of pages. Sketch out what is on each page such as buttons, graphics, links, and text. Go back to those sites you visited to get ideas, and scan through them to make sure you've included each process.

SET OUT ON THE TRAIL

How will you build your website? Here's where the road splits into three paths, and you get to choose one. No matter what path you choose, the key is to get it done. Your three options are to hire a designer, use a prepackaged solution, or be a techie and learn how to do it all yourself. If you want to learn how to do it yourself from scratch, go for it. But don't let it drag out for six months. Your decision should be based on your time, money, talent, and the complexity of your site. *Millionaire Blueprints Teen* did a quick survey of all three options and came up with the suggestions offered here. It's a good idea to establish your goals and budget before approaching this next step.

PROFESSIONAL DESIGN: USE HIRED HELP

This option offers you the most flexibility; you can do anything you and the designer dream up. It will cost you more, but often originality and professional marketing expertise will mean more sales in the long run. You can find a web designer by searching online or by checking the *Yellow Pages*, but it's best to get a referral. Ask friends or local businesses for a recommendation. You can also contact your local chamber of commerce (**www.chamberof commerce.com**), and ask for a referral. These organizations are well connected with the community, and anyone they refer you to should be reputable.

You can also find a designer online by contacting companies that created sites you like. However, you may not be able to meet them in person, so establish good communication. According to Salary.com, most web designers in the United States earn an hourly rate of $22 to $40, and some charge as much as $75 to $150 per hour. Some offer a per-page rate or a price quote based on work for the whole site. This is another good reason to map it all out before you contact a designer.

Once you find a designer, ask to see at least three samples of his or her work, and get contact information for each company. Check their references. Make a list of questions to ask before you call, and listen to the answers people give. Ask if they are happy with the service they received, whether they are still using the designer for ongoing projects, and if the designer stayed within the budget.

PREPACKAGED SOLUTIONS: RENT BIGGER TOOLS

These will save money and time, but will limit your options. Many come free with a webhosting service. They're easy to use and walk you through the process step-by-step. Templates are often used, which means your site will look similar to other existing sites. If your company is small, and you just want to get your site off the ground, this may not be an issue for you. One thing to demand (unless your site is for a hobby) is an individual web address.

Some all-in-one solution sites use your domain name in conjunction with their own. This doesn't look as professional, is too long for printing and giving out verbally, and is difficult for your customers to remember. Look through samples of websites that others have created with the system to see how well they work.

If you aren't sure whether a system is reputable, send an e-mail through the "Contact Us" link of one of their sample sites, and ask for a reference from one of their existing customers. Inquire about that customer's experience in building their site. Ask how easy the system was to use and whether they are still happy with the site.

DO IT YOURSELF: GET OUT YOUR PICKAX

If you are a techie, you may already have some knowledge of this subject and know where to begin. We recommend doing some research on marketing and making your site consumer-friendly, as this may be your weak area. One of the most popular design programs for do-ityourselfers is Adobe's Dreamweaver, available for around $400 at **www.adobe.com/products/dreamweaver**. (See the resource section for more suggestions and many useful links.)

If you don't already know hypertext markup language (HTML) or a similar design language, but are determined to learn, make sure you are doing it for the right reasons. If setting up this website is just a hobby, then go ahead. If you are starting, or building, a business (unless it is related to web design), you're better off choosing one of the other two options we mentioned previously. Your time is better spent focusing on the things you do best.

LOOK OUT FOR FOOL'S GOLD

What questions should you ask? Once your website has been built, you'll want to perform several different tests on it. Ask several friends to go online and view your site. The goal is to view it with several different browsers, monitors, and modem speeds. Make sure the pages load quickly, that all the buttons work, and that the images aren't distorted or too big (causing visitors to have to scroll around too much). Also, ask several people to read everything to catch errors in both text and numbers. If you're selling products, you want to make sure you aren't advertising something for $9.99 instead of $99.99.

This is also the time to ask others for their opinions about your site. If you have existing customers, ask them to check it out and give you feedback. If not, ask your friends and family to give their opinions. You can offer a small freebie for this service, but most people will be flattered to be asked and will do it for free. Keep in mind that you can't please everyone, so if two-thirds of your reviewers like your site that's probably enough for now.

STAKE YOUR CLAIM

What do you need to know about publishing and web-hosting? Resolving the issue of publishing and webhosting is a matter of finding a reliable service that is up and running 24/7. Installing and maintaining your own servers can cost thousands of dollars, so you'll want to find an outside source for this unless you have a huge technology budget.

Most have a set-up fee and then an ongoing monthly fee. Bare-bones webhosting and site building can be found at places like GoDaddy.com for as little as $3.99 per month. Other affordable plans allow you to set up a store with shopping cart solutions and more. Yahoo! Small Business (**http://smallbusiness.yahoo.com**) also provides web-hosting, with plans starting at $11.95 per month and a $25 set-up fee. Make sure that your webhosting service has room for expansion. As your site grows and your web traffic increases, you'll probably need to buy more webhosting space.

MINE FOR GOLD

How will you market your site and then drive traffic? With proper use of keywords and pay-per-click advertising, people are sure to find your site. But don't make those your only marketing strategies. Here are a few other suggestions to increase your traffic:

- **Actively market your site.** Print your web address on everything that carries your company name. Create an e-mail signature, or paste a link to your site at the bottom of every e-mail you send out.
- **Post free, helpful information on your site.** Are you an expert on something that relates to the purpose of your site? Write some articles about it (or hire a writer

to do it for you), and offer these articles for free to your visitors. Giving away free information always builds good will. You will also establish yourself as the generous expert, which makes people want to hire you or buy your products. Although you need to give away only the tip of the iceberg to gain interest, if you give away only one ice cube then people won't see your value.

- **Create a free e-zine with helpful tidbits.** Your list of subscribers will grow in time as people find you. Include sales pitches, or plug new items to your customers—even when they aren't visiting your site on a regular basis.

SETTLE IN FOR THE LONG HAUL

How will you maintain your site? The web, like technology, is constantly evolving—and, hopefully, your company (or whatever the purpose for your site) is evolving as well. Once your site is built, you cannot walk away and think your task is done. On the contrary, it's just beginning. It needs to be updated and maintained constantly.

Depending on how you built it in the first place (whether you did it through the self-taught method, whether it was prepackaged, or if it was professionally designed), this is probably the same method you'll choose to maintain your site as well. Just make sure you allot a regular budget of time and money for this process. If you are doing it yourself through one of the first two options, you'll want to check the site at least weekly—and more often, of course, if you're accepting orders. One sure way to make people abandon your site is not to update it regularly. And if they can't see any updates, i.e., there are no dates or other evidence of change, they'll usually move on—regardless. One way to avoid this is to post a "last updated on (fill in the date here)" line at the bottom of each page. Use one of the design tools that automatically updates the date each time you log into the page, whether you change anything or not.

This is an exciting time of exploration, when anyone and everyone is putting up a website. As with any journey, doing your research beforehand and preparing for the inevitable challenges will save countless time and money along the way. But don't let this time, and this prospect, slip away. You have the opportunity to be a part of the exploration and civilization of a new frontier.

THE RESOURCES

PC Magazine
www.pcmag.com/category2/0,4148,7488,00.asp
Check out *PC Magazine*'s picks for the top 100 classic and top 100 undiscovered websites for 2007.

How Stuff Works, Inc.
www.howstuffworks.com
Contains a whole selection of explanations related to computers and the Internet.

Librarians' Internet Index
www.lii.org/search/file/Webdesign
Offers a free newsletter featuring various websites and online information from "the best" of the web.

CHECK OUT THESE HELPFUL LINKS, AND DO SOME MORE READING ON THE STEPS OF WEB DESIGN.

Learn the Net
www.learnthenet.com/english/section/Webpubl.html
Before you begin to set up your website and choose a

domain name, peruse this website. It offers various articles of interest.

Website Pros, Inc.
www.efuse.com/index.html
Building an attractive and effective website takes practice and learned skills. This site offers free tutorials, information, inspiration, and assistance "written in plain English by professional writers and designers, so it's easy to understand and use."

WEBSITE TEMPLATES

Allwebco Design Corporation
www.allWebcodesign.com/setup/index.htm
Design ideas and countless templates are available here to help you build a truly stellar website.

Templates Box
www.templatesbox.com
Provides free and premium web templates and flash templates, website design solutions for web developers and webmasters (such as top-quality web templates, webpage layouts, logo templates), and numerous web graphics. Also offers a free newsletter and tutorials.

Adams Site Internet Services
www.adamssite.com
Serving as a directory for template designers, webpage hosting providers, and other webmaster resources, this site sells numerous web templates.

SpecialTemplates.com
www.specialtemplates.com/all_templates.htm
Offers thousands of website templates. Provides webhosting forums.

FreeLayouts.com
www.freelayouts.com/templates/display/templates
This site offers free website templates for beginners and for experienced web designers.

ALL-IN-ONE WEBSITE SOLUTIONS

GoDaddy.com, Inc.
www.godaddy.com
Offers design services, webhosting, shopping cart solutions, and more at low monthly fees.

QuickBizSites
www.quickbizsites.com
Offers website design and webhosting solutions.

Homestead
www.homestead.com
Provides website designs, e-commerce services, a design gallery, and more.

CityMax
www.citymax.com
With partnerships like Google, eBay, PayPal, and Yahoo!, this website has the reputation to back up its claim of being the "original all-in-one website builder." In addition to website design tools and templates, CityMax offers shopping cart and editing services, a huge image library, a search engine, a product auction, listing centers, domain names, webhosting, e-mail services, and complete customer support.

Yahoo! Small Business
http://smallbusiness.yahoo.com
Contains webhosting, customizable design tools, virus protection, e-mail services, search marketing, tracking, and a comprehensive help center.

WEBHOSTING

HostIndex.com
www.hostindex.com
This is an extensive directory of webhosting companies. HostIndex.com does not provide webhosting services itself. What it does offer is a ton of leads, free domain name registration, and more. Check out its webhosting glossary to become an expert on industry terminology.

HostAway.net
www.hostaway.net
Offers various webhosting and virtual private server plans, management services, reseller options, and more.

HostingServices.com
www.hostingservices.com/abcgifts
Search this listing for webhosting companies.

SHOPPING CARTS AND MERCHANT ACCOUNT LINKS

VeriSign
www.verisign.com
Conduct your e-commerce here, and gain information on industry news and events. Their global infrastructure provides the "critical layer of intelligence and security that enables key transactions, protects data, and safely delivers information across a myriad of protocols and devices."

Merchant Warehouse
www.merchantwarehouse.com
Offers credit card hardware and software, plus complete processing services.

Buyer Zone
www.buyerzone.com
Provides credit card processing, a supplier network, and more.

1Shopping Cart
www.1shoppingcart.com
Shopping cart software, Internet marketing tools, merchant accounts, autoresponders, affiliate programs, and a support center.

Quick Pay Pro
www.quickpaypro.com
An e-business automation system offering credit card processing, follow-up marketing, and an affiliate program.

LINKS TO DO IT YOURSELF

W3 Schools
www.w3schools.com
Provides dozens of free tutorials. Also offers hypertext markup language (HTML), extensible markup language (XML), and active server pages (ASP) certification programs.

Jupitermedia Corporation
Web Developer's Virtual Library
www.wdvl.com
E-commerce, webhosting, and web developer articles, plus e-books, and more.

Jupitermedia Corporation
Web Developer's Journal
www.webdevelopersjournal.com
This online journal has articles on numerous topics, including website design, HTML, graphics, webtools, webaudio, e-commerce, and more. Also offers editorials and forums.

Jupitermedia Corporation
Internet.com
www.internet.com
The network for technology professionals.

Jupitermedia Corporation
WebReference.com - Dev the Web
www.webreference.com
Collection of online articles on everything connected to the web.

Devstart, Inc.
HTML Primer
www.htmlprimer.com
Online assortment of articles pertaining to HTML and cascading stylesheets (CSS) (web design and development techniques), including how to add CSS to HTML documents.

CNET Networks, Inc.
Download.com
www.download.com
Includes numerous HTML editors and file conversion programs.

WEB DESIGN SOFTWARE

Adobe Systems, Inc.
Dreamweaver
www.adobe.com/products/dreamweaver
Dreamweaver software includes CSS tools and components for building dynamic user interfaces.

Microsoft Corporation
http://office.microsoft.com/enus/frontpage/default. aspx?ofcresset=1
The award-winning web authoring tool, Microsoft Office FrontPage was discontinued in 2006. Check out these links to find out about your software alternatives to FrontPage, including Office SharePoint Designer 2007 and Expression Web.

http://office.microsoft.com/enus/sharepointdesigner/FX1 00487631033.aspx
Microsoft suggests that you use Office SharePoint Designer 2007 if you are a solution creator and content author.

www.microsoft.com/Expression/products/overview. aspx?key=web
Microsoft suggests that you use Expression Web if you are a professional web designer.

Adobe Systems, Inc.
GoLive 9
www.adobe.com/products/golive
Adobe GoLive 9 software allows visual creativity for graphic designers and web professionals with a CSS-based content. Offers you the ability to design graphics in other applications and transfer them to the web with uncomplicated site management tools.

Trellian
InternetStudio
www.trellian.com/internetstudio
You can download this suite of software here for free. InternetStudio includes a range of tools for web authoring, e-commerce, and search engine optimization.

SOFTWARE TOOLS FOR EDITING
AND MANAGING GRAPHICS

Adobe Systems, Inc.
Photoshop
www.adobe.com/products/photoshop/family
The Adobe Photoshop family of products is the "ultimate playground for bringing out the best in your digital images and transforming them into anything you can imagine."

Illustrator CS3
www.adobe.com/products/illustrator
Do you like to experiment with color? Need the ability to work faster with new drawing tools and controls? The Adobe Illustrator CS3 software allows you to "produce artwork for print, web, mobile, and motion designs."

Corel Corporation
Paint Shop Pro Photo X2
www.jasc.com
This software helps you become a professional photographer. Offers a graphics viewer, a converter, and precision editing tools.

SEARCH ENGINE REGISTRATION

Incisive Interactive Marketing, LLC
Search Engine Watch
www.searchenginewatch.com
Find, and list, your site with individual search engines. Offers online articles, blogs, forums, and tutorials on search engine optimization.

Spinfish Media
AddPro.com
www.addpro.com
In addition to search engine registration, this site also offers website promotion, Internet marketing, search engine optimization tips, and pay-per-click services.

LEGAL AND SECURITY ISSUES

Copyright Website, LLC
www.benedict.com
Online copyright services, plus general copyright information and specialized information for webmasters.

University of California, Los Angeles (UCLA)
Online Institute for Cyberspace Law and Policy
www.gseis.ucla.edu/iclp/hp.html
Legal opinions on Internet-related issues.
(**NOTE:** This is archived information collected from the Internet's formative years, 1995 through 2002.)

www.gseis.ucla.edu/iclp/resources.html
Make sure to check out this link for a list of online cyberspace law and policy resources held in high regard by UCLA.

National Institute of Standards and Technology (NIST)
Information Technology Laboratory
Computer Security Resource Center
www.csrc.nist.gov
Offers resource links, numerous online publications, event information, and more—all pertaining to Internet security.

OTHER MISCELLANEOUS SERVICES

Bravenet Web Services, Inc.
www.bravenet.com
Offers free websites and webtools, including traffic analysis, webhosting, and affiliate programs.

Chamber of Commerce
www.chamberofcommerce.com
Contact your local office, and request business referrals if you opt to hire a professional website designer.

Millionaire Blueprints Teen *neither endorses nor recommends any of the companies listed as resources. Resources are intended as a starting point for your research.*

TAXES FOR TEENS
BY CHRIS LOTT

Many questions have come up regarding the considerations in starting a new business. For young entrepreneurs, the perceived issues can be overwhelming and may even cause them to think that it is too complicated or cumbersome to be worth it. This is usually not the case at all. Even though some thought should be given to these issues, nothing should get in the way of a great idea or a solid business plan.

In most situations where the business is going to be fairly simple, a sole proprietorship works just fine. This type of entity can be easily filed on your personal income tax return, if you have to file a return at all.

Typically, if you do not have a gross income of more than $850, you do not need to file. This is because the basic dependent standard deduction is $850. If, and when, your gross income exceeds this amount, you would need to start filing your own income tax return. With some help from your parents or a close friend, this can be easily accomplished. Remember that the filing requirement is based on income, not on age. So, if you are eight or eighteen, the requirement comes down to income. Review more details about filing income taxes from the Internal Revenue Service (IRS) at **www.irs.gov/publications/p929/ar02.html#d0e332**.

Developing a business plan should also be a consideration early on in the process. It should be a work in progress that is continually updated or revised. It is critical that you know who your customers will be, what costs will be incurred to make or produce your product, and what type of marketing will be needed to get your product out into the marketplace. These are just a few examples of items that should be addressed in your business plan. This is an important document that will provide the details about your product or service in order to persuade someone to buy from, or invest in, your business.

As a new business gets off the ground, the most important thing (besides a well thought-out business plan) is keeping track of income and expenses. Many new business owners can track income, but forget to keep track of any, and all, expenses they incur to start or operate the business. A simple spreadsheet will do the trick just fine until the business grows to a whole new level. Your income and expenses will be easily reportable on a Schedule C of your personal income tax return (Form 1040). Check out the details for Schedule C from the IRS at **www.irs.gov/pub/ irs-pdf/i1040sc.pdf**. Just make sure you keep all receipts for expenditures incurred.

Up until this time, you have not needed the help of an accountant or certified public accountant (CPA). If the business continues to grow to the point where you have employees or other more complicated issues, you may want to talk to someone with more experience in dealing with these issues. An accountant usually works on an hourly basis. Depending on the issues, and where you are located, these rates can run from $85 to $250 an hour. Many bookkeepers can answer these questions, and may work at a lower rate. See if your parents have a relationship with someone who could donate some of their time to set you on the right track.

Payroll issues involve making payroll tax deposits and filing quarterly payroll tax returns, which can be more complicated. You need to make certain, if you have employees, that you get all the payroll issues handled correctly. This is where a lot of business owners get into trouble. It can be easily avoided if you get in touch with someone who can set it up right from the beginning.

It is probably a good idea to set up a bank account in the name of the business as well. This way, if income comes in or if expenses go out, you will have a record of those items with your bank statements. It will make things easier, especially if you have waited until the end of the year to track income and expenses. This could be the start of something special, and you don't want to jeopardize it by not having your records in order. Even if you wait until the year's end to put your records together, a bookkeeper can quickly help get them in order if you need to file a personal tax return. However, it would be a good idea to keep track of things on a monthly basis so you have an idea of potential profit as you go along.

If it appears that you will need to file a tax return because the income threshold is met, you may want to know this ahead of time so you can set aside money for taxes, or even make estimated income tax payments if necessary. None of these items are a big deal by themselves, but it is not uncommon for a new business owner to be completely caught off guard about what the tax implications could be.

Whether you are considering a business to sell lemonade on the corner, to babysit in the neighborhood, or to set up a lawn mowing and landscaping business throughout your entire city, don't let perceived hurdles get in your way. Think about the items discussed, but focus on how to make the business profitable. Someone you know and trust, or an accountant, can worry about the details and prepare the necessary tax filing requirements. Knowing that the tax issues exist puts you ahead of most young entrepreneurs.

Hard work and a great idea can have a tremendous impact on your financial future. Diving in with your eyes wide open will certainly enhance the possibility of success.

CHAPTER 5

Jasmine
LAWRENCE

A bad day at the salon led to big dividends.

BUSINESS NAME(S):
EDEN BodyWorks

BUSINESS TYPE(S):
Natural Hair and Skincare Products

LOCATION:
Global

Once upon a time, Jasmine Lawrence had some serious hair trouble. The trouble was that she lost half of her hair when a chemical relaxer went horribly wrong. Instead of hiding her head in the sand, she got busy inventing an alternative. It took about six months to produce her first all-natural hair oil. In the meantime, she attended a business camp that jump-started her new company. From that camp, she learned how to develop a business plan. Well, that plan is now EDEN BodyWorks, and Lawrence is the chief executive officer.

Lawrence is up at 5:00 AM, and works well into the night. She recently brought in $50,000 in one day. So, what separates this powerful female CEO from the others? Well, for starters, she's still in high school. And though she boasts a straight A average, her primary extracurricular activity is her wildly successful natural hair and beauty products business, EDEN BodyWorks.

THE BUSINESS

Why did you start EDEN BodyWorks?

EDEN BodyWorks was driven from my own need for a natural haircare solution. My hair couldn't take the harsh chemical products. I wanted to develop unique products that were all-natural and that really worked. Unlike most products that are cosmetic in nature, my mission was to develop haircare products that actually delivered their promise of making hair stronger and healthier.

When did you begin to take the steps toward business ownership?

I founded EDEN BodyWorks after being selected to attend a business camp sponsored by Goldman Sachs and the National Foundation for Teaching Entrepreneurship. They empowered me. I was taught essential business skills and was provided access to resources to help develop and grow my business, including a host of advisers and mentors.

What kinds of things have been happening for EDEN BodyWorks lately?

EDEN BodyWorks has experienced tremendous growth with a rapidly expanding customer base. We manufacture and distribute all-natural hair and skincare products to beauty and braiding salons and to retailers. EDEN BodyWorks also has growing support from religious retailers that market our product to their members. Some have more than 10,000 members. Our products are currently being sold in eight states, and I'm working on expanding the line.

How, and why, were you selected to attend a business camp?

After completing an application that included an essay, I was selected to attend a business camp by the National Foundation for Teaching Entrepreneurship. This business camp was held at New York University, and it was truly an opportunity of a lifetime. I learned skills to launch and run my business. I was also teamed with individuals who helped me along the way.

How did you develop natural haircare products?

Initially, all of my products were developed for my own personal use. I developed them by researching and experimenting with various natural ingredients. After damaging my hair, I swore never to use synthetic products. So, I began to learn and explore the many benefits of herbs, plants, and botanicals to the human hair and skin.

My first product was a hair oil to help moisturize and grow my hair, while relieving my itchy scalp. The hair oil was a blend of natural and essential oils known for their beneficial properties. After seeing the results, I began to make other natural products.

How did you learn what ingredients work best?

It took a lot of research. I first had to understand the medicinal benefits of natural ingredients. I then used this information to start experimenting with my own hair. For example, I put tea tree oil in my shampoo and conditioner because, among other things, it helps stop itching. I tried many formulas on myself and on my family. I utilized their feedback to select the ingredients that worked best.

What is involved in packaging the products, including design, containers, labels, market research, and so on?

Well, conceptualizing is the hardest part. I want each product label and packaging to fully express the product's benefits, but I also want to remain consistent with my brand image. Different collections and types of products have a uniform design, or image, for easy consumer identification. For example, I recently updated my Peppermint Tea Tree Collection with a peppermint leaf design that unifies all the products in that collection.

I make many design mock-ups and samples before I have something I know is ready to go to final print. I also attend packaging trade shows to check the market to see what new types of packaging are available domestically and internationally.

How are you able to manufacture and distribute your products?

My manufacturing began small scale in my basement. Over time, I was able to purchase filling and labeling machines to make production faster and more efficient. With international customers and major retailers like Whole Foods Market and Wal-Mart, I now mass produce and distribute my products.

Do you contract with vendors or handle it in-house?

I do both. I produce dozens of products, and I have relationships with vendors who support me in manufacturing and distribution.

THE MARKETING

How do you market your products?

Word-of-mouth marketing is my greatest tool. Satisfied customers are elated to tell their friends and families about EDEN BodyWorks. As a spokesperson for EDEN BodyWorks, I travel to help promote my company and inspire others to turn their obstacles into opportunities. I also market through trade shows, television appearances, newspaper and magazine editorials, and e-mail marketing.

How were you able to gain support from religious organizations to endorse your products?

My church and other religious organizations support my business because they have seen the results. I am not ashamed to say that God made all of this possible for me. EDEN BodyWorks is modeled after the Garden of Eden, a perfectly natural and serene place.

How did you get your products into Wal-Mart?

While at a business conference, I was approached by a Wal-Mart representative and was given an opportunity to present my company and products to Wal-Mart buyers. During that meeting, and several others, I was able to secure a contract for nationwide distribution.

THE INTERNET

How did you set the tone for your website (www.edenbodyworks.com)?

The music on our website has been provided in partnership with Ken Ford, a renowned electric jazz violinist. I realized that we needed help designing and building our website and online store. I chose neoverve, inc., and couldn't be happier with how smooth they made the process for us.

I wanted a fast and professional way to launch EDEN BodyWorks online, and ProStores, Inc., was the answer. Instead of having to pay a hosting company and shopping cart provider, and buying additional software to build and maintain my online catalog and manage my orders, ProStores provides all of this.

THE LEGAL

What kinds of regulations are involved with haircare products? Are there rules in place for labeling products as "natural"? If so, what are they? How can you find them?

There are many regulations involved in manufacturing consumer products. The U.S. Food and Drug Administration (FDA) normally regulates products. However, it also provides guidance for consumer labeling on its website. The FDA will get involved in cosmetic products that make explicit claims to heal or cure. I also rely on my attorney to keep me up-to-date on the latest consumer safety laws.

Was product testing involved? If so, how does that work? How much does it cost?

Yes. Much of my initial testing was done on family and friends—not on animals. Before I started selling to retailers, I hired an independent lab to perform a variety of tests on the products. Some included microbiological and stability testing, and cross-interaction analysis based on ingredients. Some of these tests range between $300 and several thousand dollars.

Does the product have a Universal Product Code (UPC) bar code? How do you get a bar code?

All my products have an official UPC bar code. The first step to getting a UPC bar code is to complete a membership application for a global identification number (GS1) at GS1 US via **www.uc-council.org**. Members receive a unique, licensed number to create UPC bar codes and other GS1 identification numbers, plus many exclusive tools and resources.

THE MONEY

Where did you get the initial start-up capital?

I used my allowance to buy my first set of ingredients, plastic bottles, and other materials. At first, I just had one product called Jojoba All Natural Hair Oil that I sold to my friends. But, eventually, friends of friends were asking for the product, as were local stores. When I needed to buy ingredients and materials in larger quantities, I borrowed money from my parents and grandparents.

Was the initial investment from your parents enough?

Banks typically won't lend to minors, and credit card companies won't accept them as clients. In addition to the seed money from my parents and grandparents, some agreed to give me a line of credit of up to $200,000.

Tell us about "Oprah" money.

The first year, we made $15,000; the second year, we made $50,000. But the day after I appeared on *The Oprah Winfrey Show*, I sold $50,000 in product in one day!

THE PLAN TO FOLLOW

STEP 1

Develop a business plan.

STEP 2

Attend youth business camps.

STEP 3

Incorporate ways to gain constructive feedback.

NOTE: Lawrence suggests asking your advisers and mentors, as well as your family and friends, for feedback.

STEP 4

Attend packaging industry trade shows.

STEP 5

Obtain a UPC bar code.

STEP 6

Stay informed on consumer safety laws.

THE HIGHLIGHTS

- Meet mentors, advisers, and new friends at fun and informative youth business camps.
- Invent something you need for yourself. Test your ideas and products on yourself.
- Do your research, and learn from your mistakes, so you can do it better next time around.
- Experiment with your theories, and share ideas with family and friends.
- Be creative, but remember that the packaging for your product reflects on your brand image.

THE RESOURCES

EDEN BodyWorks
www.edenbodyworks.com
Jasmine Lawrence's products offer "natural solutions that integrate wellness and beauty for your hair and skin that were inspired by nature to restore and maintain the body's original design."

CAMP CEO
www.campceo.org
Programs that teach kids MBA-like concepts. A summer getaway in Carbondale, Illinois, that teaches children about negotiations, sales, customer service, and leadership.

Southern Illinois Entrepreneurship Center
www.siecenter.biz
After one week at camp sponsored by this center, kids leave with a briefcase, a business plan, and business cards.

Black Enterprise
www.blackenterprise.com
For African-American youth, this magazine has an annual Kidpreneur/ Teenpreneur Konference that teaches kids ages seven to seventeen about entrepreneurship, investing money, and developing a business plan.

National Foundation for Teaching Entrepreneurship, Inc. (NFTE)
www.nfte.com
NFTE is a nationwide non-profit based in New York that teaches kids in schools and community-based organizations how to breathe life into a business idea.

Goldman Sachs
www2.goldmansachs.com
Financial guidance can be obtained from Goldman Sachs, a "full-service global investment banking and securities firm."

THE FOLLOWING COMPANIES ARE USED BY EDEN BODYWORKS AND MAY BE USEFUL TO YOU, TOO.

neoverve, inc.
www.neoverve.com
Great for website design services.

ProStores, Inc.
www.ProStores.com
Easy, customizable e-commerce web storefront software.

GS1 US
www.uc-council.org
Everything you need to know about the supply chain standards system, GS1 US is "dedicated to the adoption and implementation of standards-based, global supply chain solutions that are open, consensus-based, and universally endorsed." Trade show information and memberships are also profiled.

PACKAGING SOLUTION

Packaging Today
www.packagingtoday.com
Online source for packaging industry news.

INDUSTRY CONFERENCE

Online Market World
www.onlinemarketworld.com
Conference and expo information, links, and schedules for anyone interested in the online supply chain.

ASSOCIATIONS

Direct Marketing Association (DMA)
www.the-dma.org
The DMA offers events, education, research, advocacy, membership, an online bookstore, and numerous other resources.

Millionaire Blueprints Teen *neither endorses nor recommends any of the companies listed as resources. Resources are intended as a starting point for your research.*

HOW TO SELL ON EBAY

STEP 1

Register and set up a seller's account on eBay. Go to **www.ebay.com**, and click on "Register." You will be asked to create a password and provide valid credit/debit card information in order to get started. If you'd rather not provide your banking information, you can become ID-verified instead. If you want to use PayPal—an easy way to accept buyers' credit cards and electronic check payments online—eBay recommends setting it up before listing your first item for sale.

STEP 2

Fill out the "Sell an Item" form. This is where you will create your eBay listing. With its specially created audio tour of selling, eBay gives you step-by-step instructions on how to choose a selling format, select a category, write a title, give an item description, decide on pricing and duration, select item location, and submit payment and shipping information.

STEP 3

Submit your listing. Make sure you are satisfied with your listing. Your listing begins!

STEP 4

Communicate. Once your buyer has checked out, eBay will notify you via e-mail. When your listing ends, remember to communicate with your buyer.

STEP 5

Receive payment. If your buyer paid with PayPal, you will receive an e-mail confirming payment. If PayPal isn't registered under your name, you will be asked to register to accept the payment.

STEP 6

Ship the item. After receiving payment, pack the item carefully and ship it to the buyer.

STEP 7

Leave buyer feedback. Always be sure to do this because it helps create a trustworthy environment, and this information will be important for other sellers.

If you want to know more about selling on eBay, you will find these steps and additional information at **http://pages.ebay. com/help/sell/sell-ov.html**.

The "Sell an Item" form can be overwhelming when you list your first auction. There are many options to choose from and a lot of information to read. So, eBay suggests that you sell one small item first to get acquainted with the service. Once you better understand the selling process and get feedback from a buyer, it will all begin to make more sense. As soon as your seller account is set up, you can start listing auctions by clicking on the "Sell" link found at the top of most eBay pages and following the instructions.

A special tip that *Millionaire Blueprints Teen* found when visiting the eBay website is that their community help boards (**http://pages.ebay.com/help/newtoebay/community-helpboards.html**) can be used to contact other sellers for advice. Many, if not most, experienced sellers are very open to sharing their valuable knowledge and tips.

Millionaire Blueprints Teen *neither endorses nor recommends any of the companies listed as resources. Resources are intended as a starting point for your research.*

MAKE FRIENDS WITH PAYPAL

Most people know that PayPal is an online payment option that allows you to accept credit card payments from your customers more cost-effectively, with no set-up or monthly fees, and with low transaction fees. According to **www.paypal.com**, this service allows you to get paid securely, because it is backed by an industry-leading fraud prevention system and effective risk management models.

If you want to use PayPal to send and receive credit card payments for your business, just go to **www.paypal.com** to set up a free PayPal business account. With this account, you'll be able to receive credit card payments and send payments to anyone with an e-mail address under the name of your business.

When you visit **www.paypal.com**, just choose the "What Is PayPal?" option. The step-by-step sign-up instructions will first ask you to choose the country where your business is located from a drop-down menu. From there, you just enter your personal and payment information (as requested) in its easy fill-in-the-blank format, and click "Submit." Then, you're all set! The site will also tell you that adding the PayPal option into your existing website's checkout is simple, and it offers a merchant integration team to assist you.

Accepting credit card payments is not all PayPal can do for you, *Millionaire Blueprints Teen* discovered after some investigation. Because of its reputation and ease of use, PayPal also promises to attract more customers, create a more global market for your products, and provide a wide range of tools to help you manage your online business.

PayPal is one of the world's largest online payment services. Its data also suggests that it is preferred by proven online buyers and that it may help you attract new customers.

With a secure global network, PayPal also allows you to buy and sell in multiple currencies, and it promises that this feature couldn't be easier or faster to use. When PayPal buyers want to pay for purchases in a selected currency, the payment is automatically converted, and there is no need to hold a balance in another currency to send a payment. Sellers can accept payments directly in a selected currency, with no currency exchange costs when they withdraw funds from their local bank accounts. You can even manage multiple currency payments using one PayPal account.

PayPal also offers a wide range of free tools to manage your online business. To take a look at these, go to **www.paypal.com**, select the "Business" tab, and then click on "Merchant Services." Many tabs lead to demonstration viewing options. Explore the other links on that page to see if PayPal is right for your business.

HOW TO GET YOUR PRODUCT IN WAL-MART

Millionaire Blueprints Teen contacted Wal-Mart, and here's what we found out. If you have a product that you would like to sell in their stores, you actually can walk into your local store and get your product placed. Once you do that, any store can request your product.

To start in your local store, simply obtain a Local Supplier Questionnaire from a Wal-Mart manager after they review your product(s) and decide they want to sell them. You can obtain the questionnaire from any store, or you can go to **www.walmartstores.com** and click on the "Suppliers" link, which will provide all the details you need.

The questionnaire must be filled out completely. The store manager and/or the district managers (for general merchandise), and the food merchandisers should sign the questionnaire and list the store numbers (by district) requesting the product.

Then, you submit the completed questionnaire directly to the Local Purchases Department at the home office.

Wal-Mart Home Office
Wal-Mart Stores, Inc.
Attn: Local Purchases Department
702 Southwest Eighth Street
Bentonville, Arkansas 72716-0145

THE DIFFERENCE BETWEEN A COPYRIGHT, A TRADEMARK, AND A PATENT

You can apply the trademark or service mark symbols to your unique word, name, or symbol. You can protect the trademark by registration through some state governments for protection only within the state in which your business is located, or through the United States Patent and Trademark Office (USPTO) for protection on a nationwide basis.

For more information on trademarks, visit the USPTO website at **www.uspto.gov**, or call and speak with a representative at 800-786-9199. To find out if someone has already registered a trademark or service mark, look it up on the USPTO trademark database online at **http://tess2.uspto.gov**.

As is the case with trademarks, you can apply a copyright symbol to your work at any time. But to legally protect your work, you must register. Registration gives you protection for your lifetime, plus seventy years. Simply fill out a form, and pay for your copyright registration. The basic filing fee is forty-five dollars, and the electronic filing fee is thirty-five dollars. The fees were in effect as of July 1, 2007. Include a copy of your work, and mail it to:

Library of Congress
U.S. Copyright Office
101 Independence Avenue, Southeast
Washington, D.C. 20559-6000

A patent gives an inventor the exclusive right to reap the full financial benefits of a product. If you think you have an item that should be patented, experts agree that hiring a competent patent attorney is the way to go.

For more information on copyrights and patents, visit the United States Copyright Office website at **www.copyright.gov**, or call the Copyright Public Information Office and speak with a professional at 202-707-3000.

THE FACTS ABOUT FRANCHISING

Did you know that it is possible to hire a firm to find franchise buyers, just as you would hire a headhunter to help with your career? As Margo Sloan, creator of a model franchise business called Dry Cleaning to Your Door (DCTYD), says, these firms charge approximately $10,000, and they can put you in touch with qualified buyers if you don't want to do that legwork yourself. Like all savvy businesspeople, these firms are interested in making the sale and moving on. And, as a buyer, you have rather limited access to available franchises because many franchise owners would rather not pay the fee.

Sloan debunks the myth that franchisors make big bucks on the initial franchise fee.

"A DCTYD franchise costs $24,500, but all is not as it appears," she says. "First, the buyer receives $4,500 in product from us for paint, logos, bags, and more—so, we're quickly down to $20,000. Then, we conduct training, send our business development directors to them for a week, and respond to them daily for the first six months. We have to do this because they have lots of questions. That's all valued at $5,000—so, now we're down to $15,000. A franchisor makes money on a ten-year relationship and sustained royalty fees. Ours is not a get-rich-quick situation."

The relationship matures into a marriage of sorts, with both parties seeing results. "Every month, the franchise owner pays us 4.5 percent of his or her gross profit," Sloan says. "If an owner brings in $20,000 a month, that's $900 a month to us. Much of that income goes to run our company, including salaries of business development directors, new programs, and other support. Plus, we pay rent, electricity, and salaries for four full-time employees. Starting a franchise incurs cost. We want our owners to succeed in the beginning and for the long haul."

CHOOSING A NAME
FOR YOUR FRANCHISING BUSINESS

The name of your business should convey the right message and be suitable as well.

After selecting a name, make sure it is not in use by another company by searching the following database:

USPTO
http://tess2.uspto.gov
Trademark electronic search system (TESS).

You should also retain an attorney specializing in trademarks and patents. To do this, search the Internet or your local *Yellow Pages*. One such resource is:

LegalZoom
www.legalzoom.com
Services include a comprehensive trademark search and an attorney locator.

NOTE: If you are not using your real name, you will be required to file a fictitious business name statement (also called a "Doing Business As" [DBA]) with your county clerk.

THE LETTER OF THE LAW: UNIFORM FRANCHISE OFFERING CIRCULAR (UFOC)

As with most types of businesses, franchising has federal laws and regulations. In addition, most states have rules and regulations to protect both the franchisor and the franchisee. For states where laws are not explicit, the Federal Trade Commission (FTC) (**www.ftc.gov**) has established a code of regulations that are generically referred to as the Franchise Rule. Part of this rule dictates that franchisors are required to provide a prospective franchisee with a detailed disclosure statement called the Uniform Franchise Offering Circular (UFOC).

The UFOC was adopted by the North American Securities Administrators Association (NASAA) (**www. nasaa.org**) in 1993 and was approved by the FTC in 1995. The states that require franchisors to register using the UFOC format (versus the FTC's Franchise Rule format) are California, Illinois, Indiana, Maryland, Minnesota, New York, North Dakota, Rhode Island, South Dakota, Virginia, and Washington. Because the registration states do not accept the FTC's Franchise Rule format, which is less stringent than the UFOC format, the UFOC format is most widely used. The FTC requires that a disclosure document be used in all non-registration states.

DISCLOSURE REQUIREMENTS

There are twenty-three categories of information that must be provided by the franchisor to the prospective franchisee at least ten business days prior to the execution of the franchise agreement. These categories include:

Franchisor (predecessors and affiliates)
Business experience
Litigation
Bankruptcy
Initial franchise fee
Other fees
Initial investment
Restrictions on sources of products
Franchisee's obligations
Financing
Franchisor's obligations
Territory
Trademarks
Patents, copyrights, and proprietary information
Obligation to participate in the actual operation of the
    franchised business
Restrictions on what the franchisee may sell
Renewal, termination, transfer, and dispute resolution
Public figures
Earnings' claims
List of franchise outlets
Financial statements
Contracts
Receipts

For more information on laws and regulations, visit the Federal Trade Commission's website at **www.ftc.gov**. Conduct your own research on the Franchise.com website (**www.franchise.com**), a comprehensive resource on the franchising industry. To download the UFOC, visit the NASAA website at **www.nasaa.org** and search for "Uniform Forms."

CHAPTER 6

CHRIS
FAULKNER

The host with the most.

BUSINESS NAME(S):
C I Host, Inc.

BUSINESS TYPE(S):
Webhosting and Data Center Provider

LOCATION:
Dallas, TX; Los Angeles, CA; and Chicago, IL

By the time he was nine years old, Christopher Faulkner had taught himself to rebuild computers and design software. A computer consultant at age fourteen and a business owner at age fifteen, the industrious high school student hired his grandparents to manage two enterprises he had built. It was with this entrepreneurial spirit that Faulkner, while he was still a teenager, was well on his way to building a multimillion-dollar web-hosting business.

With $250,000 in seed capital from the sale of early business ventures, Faulkner started Creative Innovations, a web design firm, during his freshman year at Southern Methodist University in Dallas. In the early days of his business, the young entrepreneur quickly saw a need to manage newly designed websites for his customers. Faulkner began his webhosting business working as a "one-man show" from his college apartment, which was set up with multiple phone lines. He says that he printed up to 10,000 invoices a day by himself, had no bank loans, no investors, and very low overhead. Within his first six months in business, he realized revenues of $70,000 and was able to afford a small office for his cyberspace enterprise.

One year later, in 1999, Faulkner's newly named webhosting company, C I Host, Inc., opened its data center doors. During the next four years, C I Host (**www.cihost.com**) not only doubled its customer base, but it also profited from a 690-percent revenue growth, enabling the company to expand to Los Angeles and Chicago.

Today, Faulkner's company is the largest privately held webhosting company in the world, employing more than 200 people and serving 215,000 clients in its 35,000-square-foot headquarters in Bedford, Texas. Faulkner, now age thirty, has expansion plans in the New York City market and in London.

Faulkner says that with patience, determination, and less than $1,000 in upfront capital, anyone can open a webhosting business.

"Starting simple as a reseller is the key," he advises. Faulkner was both enthusiastic and patient while explaining the technology behind his formula for success. He shared with Millionaire Blueprints Teen what it takes to set up a webhosting business in a cost-effective manner, how to obtain and keep customers, market products, and how to expand a business into the future.

THE BUSINESS

Tell us about the first two businesses you started in high school.

When I was fourteen years old, I met a man on an Internet bulletin board system who had written a program that valued baseball cards. I collected baseball cards, so I decided to have him value my collection. I bought the man's program for a very small amount of money I earned from consulting, and I started a business called ScoreBoard Enterprises in Bedford. I then bought more cards and marked them up for resale. My grandmother ran the business for me. I sold that business two years later for $100,000. This provided financing for my second venture, Central Amusement Company, which eventually became the third largest vending and arcade company in Texas. I was still in high school, so I hired my grandfather to run that business. Shortly after graduation, I sold it for $250,000. This provided the money to open my data center.

Let's start with the basics by explaining webhosting for our readers.

Webhosting is a service that allows users to post webpages to the Internet. A webhost, or hosting service provider, is a business that provides the technologies and services needed for websites to be viewed on the web. Webhosting is a primary service that consumers can utilize after obtaining either dial-up or broadband access to the Internet.

What gave you the idea to start a webhosting company?

I wanted to start a business I could manage while I was still in college and not have to rent office space. My interest has always been in computers. I founded Creative Innovations for the purpose of designing websites.

The companies that wanted websites in the early Internet usage years took a hands-off approach. They wanted someone to take care of administration, operation, and everything else associated with the site. They'd say, "Here's the money. Go do it." I quickly realized that this webhosting market would be a recurring revenue model, because I was getting a monthly check from these customers just for maintaining their websites.

So, from Creative Innovations, you shortened the company name to C I Host?

Yes. Actually, I launched a spin-off of Creative Innovations called Creative Innovations Host. I later shortened the name to C I Host for simplicity.

Tell us about your first home office and how you ran the business in the beginning.

I had several telephone lines set up in my college apartment. This was easily arranged through my local telephone service provider at a minimal cost. I wanted businesses to think that I had a large company, so I would use different names and pretend to be different employees of C I Host. I would say, "Hello, this is Joe in technical support." Sometimes I would say, "Hello, this is Chris in technical service." Or I'd say, "This is Mark in sales." The customers didn't even notice that the voice was the same. I was doing everything, including billing, for over three years. I would do all the technical support as the calls came in, which was twenty-four hours a day. I would answer sales e-mails in the morning, set up new accounts in the afternoon, then process all the billing in the early evening—all the while taking phone calls, answering e-mails to other "departments" and doing all the other things that came with starting a new business.

Sounds fairly complicated, not to mention exhausting. What type of training would a person need to start a webhosting business?

If you are going to be hands-on in this business (where you wear most of the hats), you have to understand how computers work and also understand a couple of different operating systems. In webhosting, the operating system Unix has an 85-percent to 90-percent dominance over Microsoft Windows—not just in C I Host—but overall. Apart from that, hardware knowledge of how computers work is a requirement.

Could you explain why the Unix operating system is used more than Microsoft Windows in webhosting?

Unix is an open source operating system that is freely available to anyone who wants to add to, or improve, its functions. As a result, there has been a massive number of virus fixes, new features, and additional developments over the last couple of years. There is also a lot of free software out there for Unix. Windows Advanced Server is very resource-intensive, meaning it will require a generous allocation of expensive software and hardware.

How did you learn about Unix?

I bought books at Barnes & Noble when I first got started in 1996. Two of those books were *Unix for Dummies* and *Unix for Dummies Quick Reference.*

Besides Unix, what else do you need to learn before starting a webhosting business?

Once you learn Unix, there is another piece called the web server side, which spawns the webpages. That software on Unix is called Apache Web Server. There is *Unix for Dummies* and also an *Apache Server for Dummies*. There are numerous free tutorials on the Internet for learning both. You can find these at the YoLinux Information Portal (**www.yolinux.com**) and at the Apache Software Foundation (**www.apache.org**).

Do you have to be a computer wizard to start this type of business?

No. You do, however, need the will, some aptitude, and dedication to see it through. A lot of patience is needed for this job. Computers don't always cooperate.

How did you develop your idea from concept to online presence?

First, I had to create a business model. Back then, it was on a legal pad with a pen, just writing down ideas and notes on how I was going to create the website, what I was going to offer people, what the prices of those offerings would be, and what people were going to get for their money. After I figured out what I was going to sell them, I had to figure out *how* I was going to sell them. To do that with hosting, you've got to have servers, high-speed computers, and fast Internet connections. I couldn't afford all of that until I had a strong customer base.

How did you decide what you would offer customers in the early days of your business?

I went to all the competitor websites and printed them out. I looked at the products and services they offered. Beside each feature, I would put a check mark based on whether I would buy from them. Then, when I designed my business website, my prices were lower, and I offered more storage space than my competitors. The important thing I wanted to provide was consistent technical support.

What are the necessary components of a webhosting site?

People want to know who you are, what kinds of connections and servers you have for reliability, and what they're going to get for their money.

Where did you get your equipment to start C I Host?

I built two computers, which basically were "white boxes" with single Pentium processors.

To build a computer from scratch, what would it cost?

It depends on how much hardware you have, but the costs range from about $250 to $11,000. You can host thirty or forty customers with one that costs $250.

How did you learn to build computers?

From the time I was eight years old, I had read every book I could find on computers and the Internet. At fourteen years of age, I worked for a computer consultant company called Connor Consulting. As a bench technician there, I learned more about how to repair and build computers.

Where did you buy your parts?

I bought most of them through *Computer Shopper* magazine (**http://computershopper.com**), which, at that time, was a very thick reference for a network of computer wholesalers that sold components. The best place today to find the lowest prices for hardware is Pricewatch (**www.pricewatch.com**).

What did you do next?

I assembled my servers and shipped them to a facility in Chicago called BBN Planet. They were in the business of selling physical space in small, medium, and large chunks to webhosts. They probably had 300 people doing what I was doing. They put my servers online with their fast Internet connections behind their routers and firewalls, and I controlled the servers from here. I saved money by not building a data center in the beginning. Today, of course, all you need is a computer to be a reseller for a webhosting company that has a data center, like C I Host. Searching DevStart, Inc. (**www.hostreview.com**) is a good place to start, if you are considering reselling. This site is reliable, because it reviews companies both independently and from reader input.

What types of businesses comprise your market?

Our target market always has been small to medium enterprises—those with fewer than fifteen employees.

Why did you target small- to medium-sized businesses?

The small to medium enterprise, or SME, always has been our "bread and butter," because there are so many of them out there. I would rather have 200,000 customers paying me $20 a month than 1,000 customers paying me $50,000 a month. That way, when we lose a customer to attrition, we aren't hugely affected by it due to our volume of customers. Now that we've proven ourselves in that market, it's easier to go after the larger enterprise customer.

How did you develop a customer base?

I launched a website to get people to sign up for my services and offered webhosting services at a very reasonable rate.

What was your pitch?

My pitch was "More bang for the buck!" C I Host gives you more features for less money. Back in 1996, that was a critical sales pitch, and it kind of changed the way people did business in the industry.

Specifically, how did it change the industry?

If you go to Internet Archive (**www.archive.org**), and look up all the webhosting companies from 1996 to 1997, they were giving you 25 megabytes (MB) of space for thirty dollars a month.

I looked at marketing a different way. What would people store on a server that takes up 25 MB in 1997? The answer was "nothing." If they can't do anything with 25 MB, they sure can't do anything with 250 MB. So, I offered 250 MB—ten times what my competitors were offering, at twenty-seven dollars a month.

How could you afford to do that when your competitors couldn't?

We used virtual partitions.

Can you explain that to us "nontechies"?

Sure. It's like sharing. Imagine if you have an office building, and the whole office building is on one floor. There's this huge, open room, and that office floor is the partition. You break up that partition in smaller chunks based on how much you want the customer to be allotted. The whole partition is the whole computer hard drive. If you had 100 customers on there, and they all wanted 1 megabyte of space, you'd need a 100-megabyte hard drive to put them on there. If you use a virtual partition, you could have 500 customers who wanted 1 megabyte of space and not need a 500-megabyte drive, because they share that one hard drive. We all know that customers don't use that amount of space for a website. Back in 1997, the average site used one-half of one megabyte. Today, it is under 100 megabytes and sometimes much smaller.

So, you offered them something that didn't cost you anything extra, and something that they weren't going to use to begin with. How did people find out about this great deal you were offering?

By e-mailing owners of other websites who sold business-related products and asking them to link to us. They linked to us for free, and I would link back to them. So, essentially, I had a page of partners on the website. The biggest thing that helped us was viral marketing (word-of-mouth advertising). When I got a little money from my first customers, I took out banner ads on the Internet.

How did you make the banner ads, and how much did it cost?

I went to WebHostLists.com, the only website at the time that focused on webhosting companies. Today, there are about 2,000 sites like this, which you can find by searching for "webhosting" on the Internet. I created the banner ads myself with a software program called Ulead Photo-impact (**www.photoimpact.com**). At that time, it cost me $49, and it came with a free graphic innovator. What I did was make banner images on my computer. I e-mailed the images to the companies, and they put them on their websites for approximately a $300 fee.

How do you link to someone else's website and vice versa?

You contact the company you want to link to, and then make a graphic, or a hyperlink, that your web browser sends to their website. They do the same thing.

Is there an Internet site to help us learn this?

There are many, but a good one is a company called Computer Technical Tutorials & More (**www.techtutorials.info**). Another is called the HTMLCenter, and its online tutorials are free (**www.htmlcenter.com/tutorials/tutorials.cfm/52/HTML**).

When did you move into a business office?

In 1998, I leased a 2,000-square-foot space in Bedford. The following year, I opened our first data center.

Tell us, step-by-step, how you built that first data center.

I converted the 900-square-foot sales office of our corporate office by gutting it and taking it down to just a shell space. I ordered one fiber-optic Internet connection from our phone company. I decided against raised floors, and used just normal white, square linoleum tiles to save money. We initially used the air conditioning that came with the building. After we laid the floor, we bought Telco racks, and installed those to hold the servers. Some people call these relay racks or cabinets. We purchased our first router off eBay, which saved a bundle of money.

How much are Telco racks, and where can you buy them?

When I started, the two-post racks ranged from $125 to $150, and I paid $800 to $1,500 for four-post racks. One of the biggest manufacturers is Chatsworth Products, Inc., for your storage solutions (**www.chatsworth.com**).

As far as equipment, what are the bare essentials that you would need to start a data center?

Data centers consist of just a few things: space, racks for servers, high-speed connectivity, a router, switches for the servers, and server hardware to "build the servers out" once the customers order them.

So, what do you need once you have your servers?

You need to add a level of redundancy such as air conditioning, fire suppression, additional bandwidth, carriers for fiber-optic redundancy, diesel generators (in case the power goes out), and UPSs—which stands for uninterruptible power supply—on each server. This is so the servers stay on during short power blips, and it can shield the server from line voltage spikes and drops. Remember that all of these things can come once the data center is up and making money. The essentials, like a single router, switches, just enough servers to start, and a single fiber-optic Internet connection are all you need to start up.

How do you progress in a cost-effective way from a small data center to a large one?

Instead of building a huge data center, you can start out with 1,000 or 2,500 square feet, and then expand it as customer demand warrants your expense. This is how C I Host does it: we expand in 5,000-square-foot increments once the current facility is 80-percent utilized.

Tell us about your most effective marketing strategies.

In 1999, we emblazoned the C I Host logo across Evander Holyfield's boxing trunks for his heavyweight championship bout with Lennox

Lewis. Holyfield was paid $100,000 for his services. In 2001, we sponsored the return of Howard Stern to radio station KYNG-FM in Dallas–Fort Worth. We hired a nuclear power plant worker to become a human billboard for us. He agreed to have our logo tattooed on the back of his head for five years, and we paid him $5,000 in return.

How do you maximize your profits?

We have spent lots of time developing automation and provisioning tools, so most of our new accounts are set up without a human being ever having to touch them. We renegotiate our bandwidth contracts every year to take advantage of the weak telecom market, and we keep several computer hardware vendors competing for our business all the time.

Where do you buy bandwidth, and how do you negotiate the contracts?

You go to big providers like Quest (**www.quest.com**) or XO Communications (**www.xo.com**). Most of them are long-distance carriers. You negotiate what's called a "price by megabit." You can negotiate based on how long you want your term commitment—one year, two years, and more—from your local carrier, which provides the "last mile," or local loop, you pay on distance from the carrier to your actual location. Again, they negotiate on term commitment, so work as many carriers as you can and pit them against each other. They are all hungry for business. Remember that telecom prices are falling. If you can negotiate a good price, keep the term commitment to twelve months only. This is because, in twelve months, it will most likely be cheaper. Then, you can renegotiate.

Is the current economy favorable for new webhosting companies?

Absolutely! There are a lot of players in the space, but none of them have a huge foothold as far as market share goes. There are thousands of new businesses every week registering for a Doing Business As (DBA) or Incorporation Document in the state of Texas. If you are starting a business today, you must have a website. So, if you look at one week in one state, that's an indicator of a staggering number of businesses that are starting up all over the country.

What advice would you give to someone who wants to start a webhosting business in today's economic climate?

To start out, one needs very little to become a host. Starting as a reseller may make the most sense.

Can you explain webhost reselling for us?

Simply put, reselling is a way to make money, both in the case of the provider supplying the original service—like C I Host—and the independent operator—you—doing the reselling. The reseller markets the product independently and signs up customers to the original provider's service, often providing the simple side of the service—like offering basic technical support and administration of the account.

On the service provider's side of the deal, a reselling program allows a business to expand its customer base without overextending its marketing and sales operations. C I Host has over 8,000 resellers. From those resellers, we obtain more than 300 new customers each month. Reselling allows a small, independent operator to profit from a small piece of the Internet services market without requiring a lot of technical knowledge or a big investment in infrastructure.

How do I make money as a reseller?

The profit for the reseller lies in the discount. For example, if the original service provider offers its resellers a 15-percent discount on accounts, then the number and size of the accounts it signs up would determine the money made by the reseller. In the case of a $7-per-month shared webhosting account, the reseller's cut would be about $1 per month. But in the case of a $300-per-month dedicated webhosting account, the reseller's cut would be $45 per month. The more accounts the reseller sets up, the more monthly income the reseller earns.

How can I become a reseller for C I Host?

Go to the link on our website, **www.cihost.com/products/reseller/ index.php**. Or call us at 888-868-9931 to speak with an online order specialist. You also have the option of filling out an online form, and someone will call you.

What equipment do I need?

To set up a simple reselling business, all you really need is a computer that you can use to manage the accounts and an Internet connection. With the low cost of computers today, you could start a business for $1,000 or less.

What additional expenses can I expect?

On the most basic level of reselling, you will simply be paid a referral fee for recommending the hosting services of another company and will not have to worry about paying fees upfront.

Where do I find my customers?

Your best bet is to try to attract small clients in need of beginner hosting services, like shared accounts. One of the best places to locate clients like these is to search webmaster resource sites and related message boards. From there, you can build personal relationships with them to retain their business and ensure that they recommend your services to their colleagues.

If your budget allows, you might want to try an ad campaign, either online or offline. Try pay-per-performance search engines like go2 Media (**www.go2.com**), Google's AdWords program (**https://adwords.google.com**)— or submit your website to Yahoo! for advertising (**http://smallbusiness. yahoo.com**). Eye-catching banners work. Creativity matters.

Faulkner explains why it's a great time to launch a webhosting company. "Seventy percent of our accounts are registering new domain names as businesses or starting new brands. This is a testament to the market space that's out there. I believe that, with the right attitude, marketing skills, self-education, and hard work, anyone can succeed in this business," he says.

THE PLAN TO FOLLOW

STEP 1

Be confident in your abilities and proactive in your strategies.

NOTE: Faulkner says, "Starting simple, as a reseller, is the key," and with patience, determination, and less than $1,000 in upfront capital, anyone can open a webhosting business. Remember, you may have to wear many hats in the beginning, such as sales, marketing, management, production, and accounting.

STEP 2

Get training in the webhosting business and its required software.

NOTE: Faulkner stresses the importance of understanding how computers work, and understanding a couple of different operating systems—mostly Unix. "In webhosting, hardware knowledge of how computers work is a requirement. Once you learn Unix, there is another piece called the web server side, which spawns the webpages. That software on Unix is called Apache Web Server," he says.

STEP 3

Develop your idea from concept to online presence. First, create a business model. Start by writing down ideas and notes on how you're going to create the website, what you're going to offer people, what the prices of those offerings will be, and what people are going to get for their money. Then, figure out what you're going to sell, and *how* you're going to sell your offerings.

NOTE: Faulkner says, "To do that with webhosting, you've got to have servers, high-speed computers, and fast Internet connections." You may not be able to afford all of that until you have a strong customer base.

STEP 4

Use preexisting social networks to produce increases in brand awareness. Create a page of partners on your website through word-of-mouth advertising. This is referred to in the industry as viral marketing.

NOTE: Faulkner advises that you e-mail owners of other websites who sell business-related products, and ask them to link to your website. He says, "You contact the company you want to link to, and then make a graphic or a hyperlink that your web browser sends to their website. They do the same thing."

STEP 5

Purchase only essential equipment needed to start a data center in the beginning like office space, racks for servers, high-speed connectivity, a router, switches for the servers, and server hardware to "build the servers out" once the customers order them.

NOTE: Once you can afford it, that's when you purchase air conditioning, fire suppression, additional bandwidth, carriers for fiber-optic redundancy, diesel generators, and an uninterruptible power supply.

STEP 6

Keep vendors competing for your business. This will end up maximizing your own profits. Always renegotiate term commitments with your providers—for example, bandwidth.

STEP 7

Build your customer base. Start by attracting small clients in need of beginner hosting services, like shared accounts.

NOTE: Faulkner says, "One of the best places to locate clients like these is to search webmaster resource sites and related message boards. From there, you can build personal relationships with them to retain their business and ensure they recommend your services to their colleagues."

THE HIGHLIGHTS

- Before spending the money to create a webhosting business, consider starting as a reseller instead.
- Have aptitude, dedication, and a lot of patience. Computers don't always cooperate.
- Research your competitors. Provide better products and lower prices.
- Learn all you can from books, the Internet, and stepping-stone jobs.
- All you need is a computer to be a reseller for a webhosting company that has a data center.
- Prove yourself by working in the small- and medium-sized markets first. Then, go after the larger enterprise customers.
- Be creative, and do what your competitors can't do—whether it's product, price, or customer support.
- Remember that eye-catching banners work, and strategic creativity matters.

THE RESOURCES

C I Host, Inc.

www.cihost.com

Chris Faulkner is the founder, president, and chief executive officer (CEO) of this webhosting giant that serves 330,000 domains worldwide. Providing operating data centers and working with high-profile partners, C I Host also remains an industry leader in the reselling field.

C I Host Youth Scholarship

www.cihost.com/about/scholarship/index.php

Looking for a college scholarship in technology? Check out this youth scholarship program to increase your chances of becoming part of the next generation of technology leaders.

Want to become a reseller for C I Host?
www.cihost.com/products/reseller/index.php
Client Services: 888-868-9931
Just fill out their online contact form, or call and speak with a representative.

International Data Corporation (IDC)
www.idc.com
Provides global market intelligence and financial forecasts. From the homepage, click on the "Research" tab for an extensive list of topics.

WHAT TO KNOW

A LARGE NUMBER OF HOSTING SOLUTIONS ARE PROVIDED ON THE UNIX (LINUX) PLATFORM. THIS PLATFORM IS DESIGNED TO ACCOMMODATE HEAVY WEB TRAFFIC AND SERVER LOADS. UNIX SERVERS ARE ROBUST AND ARE RECOGNIZED FOR THEIR ABILITY TO HOST MULTIPLE SITES. MORE INFORMATION OR A FREE UNIX TUTORIAL MAY BE FOUND ON THE FOLLOWING WEBSITES.

Linux Tutorial
Linux/Unix Tutorial Site
www.ctssn.com
Provides tutorials to guide you step-by-step so you can teach yourself these programs.

CMP Media, LLC
Network Computing
www.networkcomputing.com/unixworld/unixhome.html
Site consists of archived articles and information pulled from *UnixWorld* magazine.

Levine, John R., and Margaret Levine Young. *Unix for Dummies,* 5th ed. New York: Wiley Publishing, Inc., 2004.
Although Chris Faulkner read the original when he started his research,

the book cited above is the current edition. This series of books has been the standard for beginning reference on Unix for a decade. Make sure to check out the *Dummies* official website for more reference books at **www.dummies.com**.

Levine, John R. and Margaret Levine Young. *Unix for Dummies Quick Reference*, 4th ed. Foster City, CA: IDG Books Worldwide, Inc., 1998.

MORE THAN HALF OF THE WEBSITES ON THE INTERNET ARE USING APACHE, THUS MAKING IT MORE WIDELY USED THAN ALL OTHER WEB SERVERS COMBINED.

The Apache Software Foundation
www.apache.org
Community of developers and users; site offers help for open source software projects.

ApacheServer.com
www.apacheserver.com
For more information, or to purchase Apache software and hardware, check out this website.

Coar, Ken A. L. *Apache Server for Dummies*. Foster City, CA: IDG Books Worldwide, Inc., 1998.

YoLinux Information Portal
www.yolinux.com
Provides online training, countless guides and tutorials, and links for Linux users.

Amazon.com, Inc.
www.amazon.com
Search this site, and discover dozens of publications about Unix and Apache Server software.

Microsoft Corporation
www.microsoft.com
Microsoft FrontPage has been discontinued. Instead, check out Office SharePoint Designer 2007 (automated business processes) and Expression Web (website design) for all your software needs.

PhotoImpact.com
www.photoimpact.com
Do you want to create banner ads yourself? Go to this site, which is a search database, and check out the many variations of the Ulead Photoimpact software programs.

Computer Technical Tutorials & More
www.techtutorials.info
Technical information directory and tutorials, plus assorted products.

HTMLCenter
www.htmlcenter.com/tutorials/tutorials.cfm/52/HTML
Provides free tutorials for viral marketing (linking) and many more topics, plus forums, reviews, a blog, and technical job postings.

WHERE TO GO

CDROM-Guide.com
www.pcforum.com
This is a virtual PC forum trade show. Site also offers a free mailing list on all types of digital storage topics.

TechExpo Corporation
www.techexpo.com
Online exposition for technology wizards and beginners alike. Everything you'd expect to find at an industry event is showcased here.

TechFest.com
www.techfest.com
Offers electronics, computer hardware and software, and special-interest networking.

Web Host Industry Review, Inc.
www.thewhir.com
Provides information on webhosting events, and offers access to web-host interviews, blogs, news, and more. The *Web Host Industry Review* magazine can be ordered at no cost.

WHO TO KNOW

The Independent Computer Consultants Association (ICCA)
www.icca.org
Professional association of information technology consultants who offer implementation, strategic planning, support, business analysis services, and training.

JobServe USA Corporation
www.computerwork.com
Check out this website for nearly 7,000 information technology (IT) jobs, including consulting positions.

Association Resources
http://association.org
Compilation of various industry associations—all in one searchable online database.

go2 Media
www.go2.com
Provides free local search for mobile phone users. Inquire about placing ads with them.

Google
AdWords
https://adwords.google.com
Display your ads on Google and its advertising network (based on a pay-per-performance program where you only pay for the service when someone clicks on your ad).

Yahoo!, Inc.
http://smallbusiness.yahoo.com/
Advertise through Yahoo!. Check out the small business services here.

SITES TO SEE

Whois?
www.whois.com
This searchable database contains information about networks, net-working organizations, domain names, and the contacts associated with them for the .com, .org, .net, .edu, and ISO 3166 (country and territory codes) top-level domains.

DevStart, Inc.
www.hostreview.com
Research this site if you are considering reselling. It reviews companies both independently and from reader input for webhosting and virtual private servers. Also offers hosting forums, articles, various guides, and more.

WebHostLists.com
www.webhostlists.com
Search this database, and find a webhost near you.

Internet Archive
www.archive.org
Want to search archived information from the Internet's past? Check out this site, and click on the "Web" tab to get your research.

WHAT TO DO

BILLING SOLUTIONS AND SOFTWARE

PayPal
www.paypal.com
Provides online payment solutions, including credit cards, buyer credit or account balances, and bank accounts—all with your financial informa-tion hidden from hackers.

2Checkout.com, Inc. (2CO)
www.2checkout.com
Provides e-commerce solutions focused on financial reporting, affiliate tracking and sales tracking, and fraud prevention.

SpeedFox Reliable Web Services
www.speedfox.com
Various webhosting plans, including programs for all your e-commerce automation needs.

Hosting Controller
www.hostingcontroller.com
Offers hosting automation solutions for Windows-based webhosts.

AUTOMATED ORDER PROCESSING

WHM.AutoPilot, LLC
www.whmautopilot.com
Webhost management news, promotions, tips, support, and more.

ModernGigabyte, LLC
www.modernbill.com
Billing software and automation for webhosts.

WEBHOSTING SUPPORT SYSTEM

cPanel, Inc.
www.cPanel.com
Hosting and branding services, a forum, and news.

THINGS TO GET

Chatsworth Products, Inc.
www.chatsworth.com
The place to buy Telco racks to hold your servers. Some people call these relay racks or cabinets. Offers a full range of products for storage and safety in addition to cabinets and racks, including seismic protection,

grounding and bonding, monitoring and security, power management, cable runways and trays, wall-mount systems, cable management, zone cabling and wireless enclosures, and more.

BANDWIDTH

Quest Software
www.Quest.com
In addition to software for migration, provides application and database management and more.

XO Communications
www.xo.com
Offers telecom services with numerous products to fit your system's needs.

HARDWARE VENDOR AND REFERENCE PUBLICATION

Pricewatch
www.pricewatch.com
Lists price comparison of electronics and component parts with real-time quotes.

SX2 Media Labs, LLC
Computer Shopper
http://computershopper.com
In addition to the print copy of *Computer Shopper* magazine, this site offers a digital copy, buying guides, newsletters, forums, and much more.

GENERATORS, POWER CONVERTERS, AND OTHER HARDWARE

American Power Conversion Corporation
www.APC.com
Many products and accessories, including cooling systems and surge protectors, plus various software and firmware, batteries and upgrades, and support services.

Power Pro-Tech Services, Inc.
www.generator.com
Generator services and equipment sales.

ROUTERS

Cisco Systems, Inc.
www.cisco.com
Provides training and support services, event information, product research tools, and various other products—including routers.

Juniper Networks
www.juniper.net
Offers routers plus news, networking platforms, security, and many other products and resources.

WORDS TO LIVE BY

Webpage: A document on the World Wide Web, identified by a unique uniform resource locator (URL).

Web Server: A computer that serves up (delivers to your computer) webpages.

Virtual Server: A web server that shares its resources with multiple users. It's another way of saying that multiple websites share the resources of one server.

Dedicated Server: A server that has only one owner. As an owner of the dedicated server, you have full control of every aspect of the hardware and the software.

Disk Space: In a shared hosting environment, the amount of server disk storage allocated to your account.

Bit (or **Binary Digit**): A bit can be thought of as a single instruction that tells a computer processor whether it is "on" or "off." Think of this like the relationship between a light bulb and a light switch. When the switch is up, the light is on. When it is down, the light is off. A computer language combines a series of "bits" into "bytes," and provides an instruction set that tells a computer processor what to do. For a computer to translate information, it uses bits/binary digits (with a single binary value of either zero or one), which are the smallest units of data.

Byte (or **Eight Bits**): A byte is composed of eight bits or "on/off" signals in most computer systems. Computers translate instructions and manipulate bits to store, design information, and process commands in bit multiples. These multiples are called bytes.

Bandwidth: This is the pipe to your website and the data transfer capacity allocated to your webhosting account, usually measured in gigabytes (GB). One gigabyte is equivalent to 1,024 megabytes (MB).

Internet Protocol (IP): Provides the basic delivery mechanism for packets of data sent between all systems on an Internet, regardless of the systems' locations.

Operating System (OS): The operating system defines our computing experience. It's the software that enables all the programs we use—for example, Microsoft Windows.

Router: A computer on a packet-switching network that accesses packets of data from other networks and determines the best way to move each packet forward to its destination.

Colocation: A type of data center where multiple customers locate networks, servers, and storage gear.

Millionaire Blueprints Teen *neither endorses nor recommends any of the companies listed as resources. Resources are intended as a starting point for your research.*

HOW TO WRITE A PRESS RELEASE

There are three elements to any good press release: format, information, and newsworthiness. Following the format shows the media that you know what you're doing. Providing the right information is essential to getting your message across properly. Making it sound newsworthy will increase your chances of obtaining media coverage. Once you've finished crafting it, ask two or three people to proofread your press release.

FORMAT

NOTE: No two sets of instructions on how to format a press release are exactly alike, but it should look something like what is described below.

Use margins of at least 1 inch all around.

Boldface titles and heading.

Use a standard font style and size.

Skip one line between paragraphs.

Write the phrase "**FOR IMMEDIATE RELEASE:**" in all caps and bold font at the top left of your page. Be sure to include a colon after the phrase.

Below that, include all pertinent contact information: name, title, company, website address, telephone, cell phone, e-mail, and more.

Next, put the title or headline of the release in bold font.

Begin the first paragraph with your city and state, followed by a hyphen and the date you're issuing the release, followed by another hyphen. All of this should be in all caps and bold font, for example, **ARLINGTON, TX–JUNE 20, 2007–**.

Begin the text of the first paragraph on that same line.

The last paragraph could be a recap of the release or a brief company history.

After the last paragraph, list your PR representative's contact information.

If you use more than one page, type the word "more" within dashes and center it at the bottom of the page, for example, –more–. Then abbreviate the headline at the top of the next page, and include the page number. Place all in bold font.

At the very bottom of the release, type three number signs, for example, ###, and center these across the page. This tells the media that it is the end of the document.

OTHER FORMATTING INFO

Some say to double space. Others say single spacing is okay. Many experts use 12-point type and single spacing.

Some say stick to one page. Others say up to four pages is fine. It depends on the content and who will be reading the press kit.

Try not to crowd the page with words. Leave some white space to make the page more appealing to readers.

INFORMATION

Include information on who, what, when, where, why, and how in every release.

Make sure you provide several methods for people to contact you. Some people even include their home phone number since members of the media often work odd hours.

Don't overload the readers. Your goal is to get them to contact you for more information. Provide enough information so they have all the facts, but not so much that they stop reading before they reach the end.

NEWSWORTHINESS

The headline is of major importance in a press release. It should catch readers' interest and make them want to read on.

Even if you're simply doing a product announcement, try to find a news angle. Read the newspaper, and watch the news to see if there is anything you can connect it to. Scan calendars and timelines for holidays, events, and anniversaries that make your topic timely.

Media people have access to hundreds of press releases every day. To get noticed, you need to give them a reason why they would want to give you coverage. Try to find a reason why your release is important to their audience today.

For more information on writing press releases, check out PRW (**www.press-release-writing.com**), or type the words "writing a press release" into any major search engine.

HOW TO GET AN INTERNSHIP

Seth Flowerman "caught the entrepreneurial bug" at age fifteen by recognizing that he could combine his youthful insights with the organizational fundamentals of summer internships. He created Career Explorations (CE), which provides quality internships in a fun and safe environment to hundreds of high school students.

Though he is only twenty-one years old, Seth is an intern expert who has extensive experience helping students discover their passions. *Millionaire Blueprints Teen* was excited when Flowerman agreed to share some of his secrets with our readers.

GETTING IN THE BIZ

Why are you an internship expert?

Five years ago, I started a company with that specific purpose in mind! Today, as the twenty-one-year-old chief executive officer of CE (**www.ceinternships.com**), which is a $1-million-a-year business, I have helped hundreds of students experience their field of personal interest by working closely with top-flight professionals during summer internships.

When was your first internship?

During the summer preceding my junior year, I pursued an incredible opportunity that would completely change my life. With help from my parents and the father of one of my friends, I secured a financial internship with a very successful and innovative trading company involved with bonds and other financial "instruments." Working eight to ten hours a day during the summer didn't sound like my

idea of fun, but I successfully made it through several grueling interviews and flew to London to intern with the head energy trader at Cantor Fitzgerald (**www.cantor.com**).

How did that go?

Over the next five weeks, my mentor treated me like an adult. He expected that I would act accordingly, and, by the end of the summer, we had become friends who shared opinions and aspirations. I came to truly understand what it would be like to be in my chosen career field. I realized that to have the freedom to work where I chose and to live as I wanted, I would need a sharper focus and need to apply greater energy to identifying and accomplishing the steps on the path to my goals.

What did that path look like?

Over dinner, we agreed that making high-quality internships available to other students was a need begging to be filled. I learned all I could about writing business plans. I worked night and day thinking through what my company might do best and piecing together the business structure and strategies needed to accomplish the projections. My plan won first place in a national business plan competition. Winning gave me the confidence to incorporate CE. One year later—after many struggles, but a successful first CE summer—I was honored at a Washington, D.C., breakfast. The head of the U.S. Small Business Administration (SBA) (**www.sba.gov**) presented me with Junior Achievement's (JA) (**www.ja.org**) International Student Award. The audience was pleased with my acceptance speech, and I was especially honored that a movie documenting the establishment of CE was created for the event. I have discovered that I am truly passionate about student entrepreneurship.

Consider this your blueprint to finding the right internship from the internship expert.

INTERNSHIPS: AN IMPORTANT STEPPING STONE

SEEK INTERNSHIPS AND REAL WORLD EXPERIENCE

The best way to find out if an area of personal interest is worth further pursuit is through a real-world internship experience. As a teenager, there is nothing better than an internship to help you discover your passions.

MAKE SURE YOU ARE READY

Deciding to spend your summer working (potentially eight or more hours per day) can be a scary thought. Make sure you are ready to accept the responsibilities that will go along with working in a professional environment. Be honest with yourself!

STEP OUTSIDE YOUR COMFORT ZONE

Knowing that you are ready is one thing, but going outside your comfort zone and pursuing an internship takes courage. Deciding not to go back to the same summer camp that you have been to for the past seven years can be tough.

FIND INTERNSHIPS

Internship programs are available through CE at firms in Boston and New York. For a summer in London, check out internship programs through Intern Exchange International (**www.internexchange.com**). It can identify what opportunities exist and provide you with a living arrangement that is fun but also acceptable to your parents. If you decide to find an internship on your own, don't be afraid to use any resources you have available. Talk with your parents, your friends' parents, your grandparents, your college/guidance counselor, your coaches, and more. Ask them if they know anyone who might need help in the industry that you are interested in as a career. The worst thing that happens is that someone says, "No."

TAKE A RISK, AND DON'T FEAR REJECTION

There is someone out there who would love to have you as an intern—you just need to find them! Picking up the phone and calling a potential boss takes courage, but it is essential if you want to line up an internship on your own. Be prepared, polite, and persistent—if there is an opportunity, you want to be the one who gets the internship.

BE PROFESSIONAL

Remember that you will be interning in a professional organization. Your correspondence and presentation should be professional if you want to make a good impression. That means e-mails should not use acronyms like LOL. Use the word "you" instead of the letter "u." Phone conversations shouldn't include too many "likes" or "ums." Interviews must be taken seriously, so wear appropriate professional attire.

BE WILLING TO WORK WITHOUT PAY IN THE BEGINNING

Not everyone starts out as the president of the organization. An internship experience can be much more valuable than any compensation you might receive. If you absolutely have to get paid, approach the subject delicately.

FIND A MENTOR, NOT A COMPANY

Don't worry about interning with the top company in the world for a particular field. If you think you are interested in journalism, don't expect to be working for the *New York Times* or the *Wall Street Journal*. It is much more important to focus on finding a mentor who is excited about teaching you about the field and giving you the best chances to try out working in the organization.

FIND A DYNAMIC ENVIRONMENT

The best internship is one where you will be exposed to as many different areas of a given field as possible. Smaller companies often provide a more dynamic internship experience for students.

BE PROACTIVE

Go above and beyond the projects that you are given at work. Try to learn from the other people in your office and not just from the person that you are interning for. If you finish the task that you were working on, don't wait to be given another task. Instead, ask around to see if there are other ways that you can be helpful.

GET LETTERS OF RECOMMENDATION

Don't be afraid to ask for letters of recommendation near the end of your internship. Be tactful, but you may want to remind your boss/mentor about the projects that you worked on during the internship and ways that you contributed.

EMBRACE THE CHALLENGES

Understand that your challenge is to learn all you can through the internship, both the exciting and the less pleasant aspects. During an internship, you may realize that you have found the industry that you want to pursue in college or as a career. Alternatively, you may find that the field is nothing like what you thought, and that you don't want to have anything to do with that industry. Either scenario is valuable if you think of the internship as a learning experience.